Law and Governance in Islamic Societies

The Legislative, Judicial, and Executive Branches in Islam

Abd al-Wahhab Khallaf

Ahmed E. Souaiaia (Auth., Tr.)

Information @ MAJALLA.org/press/

ISBN: 979-8-88823-006-0 (Hardback)

First edition 2001, as *Profiling the Islamic Civilization*
Reprinted 2024, as *Law and Governance in Islamic Societies*

PRINTED IN THE UNITED STATES OF AMERICA

Table of Contents

Preface

This work is a translation from Arabic of two lectures by Abd al-Wahhāb Khallāf (d. 1956). The materials were originally published in Arabic in two different books. One was published in 1971 under the title *Khulāsat tārīkh al-tashrī` al-islāmī.* The other was published nearly ten years later under the title *al-Sulutāt al-thalātha fī al-islām.*

This revised translation is based on the Arabic text of *al-Sulutāt al-thalātha fī al-islām,* which was published in 1980, but is also checked against some of Khallāf's ideas published in his other works including *Ilm uṣūl al-fiqh, al-ijtihād wa-'l-taqlīd,* and *fiqh al-siyāsa al-shar`iyya.*

Foreword

Abdul Wahhāb Khallāf (1888 - 1956) was one of the most prominent jurists and experts in Sunni Islamic law. He was one of the religious and secular thinkers who contributed to building the features of the so-called conceptual edifice for Egypt in the era of liberalism, and who encouraged the appearance and participation of religious scholars in the media including radio, television, and newspaper. He was the most prominent person to address the public by radio when radio was established, and later became a public intellectual and a cultural icon.

Born Abd al-Wahhab Abd al-Wahid Khallāf, in the city of Kafr al-Zayyat in March 1888, Khallāf received a traditional religious education. After that, he joined al-Azhar in 1900. He was one of the first students to join the Sharia School since its founding in 1915, and he completed his studies there, graduating in 1915.

Khallāf became a *shaykh* (religious authority) and worked at al-Azhar's Sharia Judiciary School immediately after his graduation. He remained there until the 1919 Revolution broke out, with which he seemed to identify. During the revolution, he moved to judicial positions in the Sharia courts (1920); later he was appointed director of mosques in the ministry of endowments in 1924; in 1931 he was appointed to the Courts Inspection Department.

In 1943, Khallāf was appointed as an instructor at the Cairo College of Law. In 1936, he was selected for a professorship of Islamic law at Cairo University, where he remained until his retirement in 1948. While in retirement, the university extended his service, assigning him a teaching role in the graduate studies department, and he remained active in that capacity until his passing in 1956.

Khallaf was an active scholar inside and outside Egypt. Together with his colleague, Sheikh Mahmoud Shaltut (1893-1963), he amplified the work of the Arabic Language Academy by establishing the Islamic Research Academy to engage with scholars outside Sunni Islamic institutions. He and Shaltut were instrumental in establishing and promoting intersect dialogue among Sunni and Shi`a scholars.

In terms of his insight on *ijtihād*, he identified four conditions that must be met for one to achieve eligibility for *ijtihād*:

- Familiarity with the Arabic language and the ways in which its expressions and vocabulary are denoted;
- Knowledge of the Qur'an;
- Knowledge of the Sunna; and
- Understanding of the critical aspects of analogy.

Khallaf left an extensive body of work, all in Arabic, listed here in translated titles to signal the topic and theme of each work.

- Endowment Provisions and Inheritance Provisions (Rules of Public Trust [Ahkam al-waqf]), al-Nasr Press, Cairo, 1953.
- Guardianship of Money Law, Dar Al-Nasr Press, Cairo, 1955.
- Jurisprudence of Sharia Policy, Dar Al-Ansar, Cairo, 1930.
- Principles of Jurisprudence—Ijtihād, Dar Al-Kitab Al-Arabi, Cairo, 1950.
- Science of the Principles of Jurisprudence, al-Nasr Press, Cairo, 1942.
- Sources of Legislation for What Doesn't Have a Text, Institute of Higher Arab Studies, Cairo, 1954.
- Summary of the History of Islamic Legislation, (first printed with the book Ilm uṣūl al-fiqh, Cairo, 1942.
- Rulings on Legal Conditions in Islamic Law According to the Doctrine of Abu Hanifa and What Should be Done now in the Egyptian Sharia Courts, Al-Nasr Press, Cairo, 1936

- The Sharia Policy or the System of the Islamic State in Constitutional, Foreign and Financial Affairs, Salafi Press, Cairo, 1930
- The Three Authorities in Islam, Afaaq al-Ghad House, Cairo, 1980.

Introduction

Origins and Evolutions of Islamic Institutions

In learning institutions, scholars, researchers, scientists, experts, and professionals signal their commitment to the production of evidence-supported knowledge by qualifying their approaches, findings, or conclusions as being "critical." Yet the descriptor "critical" is too broad and vague an adjective to understand without context. Even within academic and learning institutions, "critical" could mean different and sometime contradictory things. In medicine, for example, something or someone in a critical condition would be nearing their end. Conversely, a scholar of philosophy producing a critical work has not made tired, unlively, dead, or near-dead work. Despite its popularity and broad use, the qualifier "critical" should be understood and applied properly for it to be instructive and useful.

This preface about the meaning and function of the word "critical" is needed because this is a work whose translation, below, could be readily dismissed as an "uncritical" text. Indeed, the very basic meaning of critical, as understood in the social sciences and the humanities, would apply here: It is a single perspective; an accepting, nonjudgmental, and linear telling of the story of Islamic law and governance from within a single school of Islamic thought, using a singular lens. However, such work is in and of itself critical evidence. In fact, its uncritical character, in terms of approach, is what makes it so instructive and critical in terms of substance. Its insider perspective provides an organic insight into the meanings, origins, and evolution of Islamic thought and institutions. In other words, it is not just the information about the topic that is presented, but the way this information is understood, preserved, and perpetuated tells the fuller story of how Muslim religious scholars navigated key historical events, many of which were deeply controversial and transformative. Such a narrative can help students understand the processes of knowledge production as they happen now and apply them to how they might have happened in times past.

Given the vagueness associated with being critical, I preface this uncritical work with what some might consider a critical introduction. However, from my experience, a declaration that a work is critical is not enough. It must clarify the standard by which criticality is defined and applied.

Here, as has been the case in my teaching and research activities, the framework applied to understand and analyze ideas and events defines criticality. To that end, my work must be understood as an outcome of the application of Systems Thinking framework and its relevant principles.

In the case of introducing this narrative in translation, I consider its author as part of the body of evidence of Islamic law and governance. As elements of human society, each one of us is an outcome of a plurality of systems that make us who we are and cause us to have different preferences and priorities. Muslim religious scholars, in the end, are also products of the systems that produce their identities, and it is through such identities that they see and process the world around them.

Religious scholars are preservers of tradition. For a religious tradition to persist, it must be free of blemishes that could challenge its authority. When these blemishes occur, a religious scholar's role is to de-emphasize, diminish, and relegate them to insignificant distractions. A religious scholar, like a physicist, will conveniently judge an event insignificant the same way a physicist will consider a variable insignificant when it has an impact on the calculation of a phenomenon. The strategy of dropping variables simplifies equations, and the strategy of glossing over historical events produces a linear thinking that results in an unproblematized narrative about the origins and evolution of religious ideas and institutions. However, when we consider events such as the first and second Islamic civil wars, the massacre of Karbala, the rebellions of the enslaved and the peasants, and the revolutions of the *`ulamā'*—can we really say that these were all insignificant events?

These social crises were not just isolated events driven by limited political dissent, with impact on the developmental trajectory of the religious, political, and legal institutions in Islamic societies; they were events that profoundly transformed religious discourse, so much so that they produced or institutionalized Islamic sectarianism, giving birth to Ibadism, Shiism, and Zaydism—schools of religious and legal thought that have continuously challenged the established political order since the seventh century CE.

To get a sense of how religious scholars reacted and handled events such as those described above, one can simply look at the reactions from and positions taken by various religious scholars and the religious institutions they represent in our lifetime. We can consider their reactions to the Iran-Iraq war; to the violent struggles of 2011; to the 2023-2024 war in Gaza; and to similar events. The reactions of religious scholars from the ninth century were not radically different from the reactions of religious scholars of the 21st century because, while individuals can form unique positions, human society often behaves consistently regardless of time because it reflects the will of the dominant social group, not some universal norm untouched by circumstance and social forces.

It is the collision between religious principles and social events that shatter the meaning of criticality in the production of knowledge. Religious discourse is founded on the idea that values and religious rules come from outside this world and are therefore unaffected by earthly social events, regardless of their significance. However, social events establish, beyond a doubt, that religious teachings and practices are born during turning points in history. The fact that all major religions and all sects have a birthdate underscores that religions are born during transformative social events—even if their ideas can be located on a different timeline or even in a different space.

From a Systems Thinking point of view, accounting for as many variables as possible—and applying as many of the principles of Systems Thinking as possible—is necessary to understanding any event or phenomenon. That means including religious scholars and religious conceptual and practical systems alongside timelines of significant events. In this way, this introduction is a critical introduction because it expands the space for inquiry beyond religious rituals and religious ideas, to encompass the environment and the events where ideas and rituals come to life.

The practical implication for the application of Systems Thinking to explain and analyze Islamic law and governance is to assume that events described or prescribed by Muslim religious scholars are outcomes of conceptual or practical systems and that the existence of one event had transformative effects on other events, immediately or over time.

These notes about the Systems Thinking approach create tools for producing a critical introductory chapter to a work that is meant to be consumed internally—by Muslims, for Muslims. Furthermore, the introduction reframes the examination of Islamic law and governance by inserting events that have been left out in religious discourse or events that were used to justify or codify rules and norms.

From a Systems Thinking framework, one must acknowledge the forces that inform and guide the analysis and the articulation of findings. While training and practice enable Muslim religious scholars such as Khallaf to produce a linear, unproblematized narrative about the origins and evolution of religious ideas and institutions, a narrative from someone fully preoccupied over a long time with the plight of social groups whose rights have been violated will necessarily produce a narrative that emphasizes those elements and events. Therefore, critical work and an uncritical work are not alternatives; they complement and depend on one other in order to produce a reliable, fact-based, more complete history of ideas and events.

Contextualizing Khallaf's Work

The translated work below is derived from a series of lectures on Islamic law and governance delivered by a traditional Islamic religious scholar. The audience of these lectures was likely advanced students of Islamic studies in Egyptian religious institutions. Given the setting, the information presented in these lectures lacks background information and presumes familiarity with the history of Islamic thought, events, and institutions. Khallaf presents his content linearly, descriptively, and without a critical analysis of the events that forced shifts and turns in the trajectory of Islamic thought and practices.

In contrast, the audience of this translated work presumably consists of students of Islamic and near-eastern studies in non-Muslim majority countries, and members of the public interested in learning about the origins and history of Islamic legal and political thought and institutions from the point of view of Islamic traditional scholars.

To gain the most benefit from this work, readers should have some background with which to situate Khallaf's ideas within the growing body of Islamic studies. This introduction is intended to provide a novice reader of Islamic thought with context that allows them to have a fuller picture of the long history of Islamic political, legal, and cultural legacy.

In short, this introduction is intended to provide a point of reference that allows the reader to compare the assumptions, preferences, and approaches of traditional religious scholars in their engagement with the legal and political history of pre-modern Islamic societies. In this introduction, we highlight issues which modern

Muslim thinkers and leaders have struggled to address through the lens of Islamic values. After all, explanations of classical Islamic thought and institutions seek relevance and anchor points of that tradition in a world that is no longer shaped by Islamic values the way it was before the fall of the caliphate system.

A Rights-Biased (not based) Account of the Origins and Evolution of Islamic Thought and Institutions

Islam originated in the city of Mecca on the Arabian Peninsula in the first half of the sixth century CE. The city of Mecca at that time was a trading outpost, linking Africa, Europe, and Asia. As such, Mecca became a city-state, governed by a tribal council that selected a chief from leaders of its clans, oftentimes the leader of the strongest clan. The economy of Mecca depended on trade and animal herding: mainly camels, sheep, and goats. Mecca's economy was a market economy involving local and global trade. Residents of Mecca and members of Bedouin clans who lived a traveling distance from Mecca generally traded goods for goods. Caravan owners who transported goods across continents used gold and silver coins, currencies named *dinar* and *dirham*, to carry out transactions with far-away communities. Archeological finds, poetry, and the Quran provide evidence that the inhabitants of Mecca used money and goods for trade. The market form of economy decided the kind of society Mecca could be.

Unlike the people of Madīna, a city north of Mecca by nearly 300 miles, the people of Mecca were less attached to their land and more attached to their gold, silver, and camels. A Meccan's material wealth comprised the number of camels they owned and the count of *dinars* and *dirhams* to their name. The type of economy in Mecca before Islam, being less dependent on labor and more dependent on exchange, created unique social values and social relationships. The people of Mecca placed a premium on values such as trust, loyalty, honor, and generosity—the kind of traits that emphasize family over the larger community. However, security concerns, mainly the protection of property like caravans and animals, compelled clans to enter into treaties with one another for mutual security. Quraysh, the umbrella tribal organization that governed Mecca before the rise of Islam, was a coalition of more than twenty clans.[1]

Given their dependence on intercontinental trade, Meccans needed to secure their own caravans as well as their economic interests. To realize both goals, they tolerated and even preserved what might appear as conflicting interests: transit security and plunder. People near Mecca made a living through violent raids on distant tribes and caravans. This practice was tolerated, apparently, because it kept traders from distant lands from engaging in cross-continental trade, motivating foreign traders instead to rely on locals to secure trade routes. However, when these raiders attacked clans from their own tribe—that is, members of Quraysh or of a tribe with which Quraysh had a pact—the punishment was severe.[2] These practices created a culture that tolerated and even glorified violence, shaping its social and economic dynamics.

The prevalence of violent confrontations for economic purposes commodified all that was captured during these battles and raids, including captured people. Captured fighters of defeated armies and their family members became slaves whom the victorious army owned and distributed as property among fighters or the families

---

[1] Because some clans were too small and not all were represented in the governing tribal council, historians are unsure on the exact number of clans within Mecca. The historian al-Mas`udi lists 25 clans as being part of Quraish. Others list fewer or more. A few of these influential clans and members of the tribe of Quraysh will be relevant to our discussion of the Islamic governments: Banu Hāshim (Muhammad, `Ali), Banu Zuhra, Banu Taim (Abu Bakr), Banu ʿAdī (ʿUmar), and Banu Umayya (ʿUthmān, Mu`awiyya).

[2] Arabic culture authorized discretionary punishment for those involved in highway robbery (*qat` al-ṭarīq*), which was later termed by Islamic law as *ḥirabah*, and made punishable by death according to some Islamic schools of jurisprudence.

of fighters who died in battle. Most enslaved persons were prisoners of war, captured family members of defeated armies. In addition to a large number of enslaved Arabs, in various historical records we find references to slaves listed as Abyssinian (*ḥabashī*; east African), Persian, Copt, Nubian, and Byzantine.[3] Historical sources reveal that the majority of enslaved persons before Islam were Arabs; African slaves constituted about one-third of listed totals. This ethnic or racial composition changed with the establishment of Islam as a state religion and with Muslims establishing their Islamic nation-state and governing institutions.

One of the supportable explanations for the majority of slaves being Arab in pre-*Hijra* times is that the effects of intertribal warfare often resulted in the enslavement of captives whose tribe failed to pay ransom to free them. As we can gather from the details of the second war involving Muslims, the Battle of Uhud fought between the Muslims of Madīna and the pagans of Quraysh, it was customary to bring along women and children to the battlefield, apparently to give extra motivation for fighters to win the battle. However, that also meant that when a side lost the battle, their family members, including women and children, were taken by the victor. Captured women were given to men who took part in the battle. These men either married them or kept them as concubines. This practice resulted in graded relationships based on a woman's status: A marriage could be one among equals (a free man marrying a free woman), a marriage among non-equals (one free man marrying one—or more than one—captive woman), and concubinage.[4] It

---

[3] See, for example Ibn Qutayba, *Kitab al-ma'arif*, 63; Ibn Sa'd, *al-Kitab al-tabaqat al-kabir*, 1:2:179–80; al-Tabari, *Kitab al-rusul*, 1778, 1779, 1780, 1781, 1940; Ibn Sa'd, *al-Kitab al-tabaqat al-kabir*, 3:1:26, 3:1:167, 8:153; and Ibn Hisham, *Kitab sirat rasul Allah*, 486, 999.

[4] Because anyone could fall into slavery by simply being part of an army that lost a war, slavery in Arab society did not carry the kind of stigma attached to slavery in western and US societies. For instance, a slave girl, due to various terms of marriage in Arab society, could become a powerful political force. Al-Khayzuran, a slave girl in the house of the ruling Abbasids, became the wife of al-Mahdi when he became caliph and the mother of his two sons, who also became caliphs. As

was customary to keep captured children with their mothers; a child's status was usually attached to that of their mother. If a captured woman became enslaved, so would her child; but if she was freed, or taken in marriage as free woman, her child would be freed, too.

The establishment of the Islamic state in Madīna, and the adoption of Islamic traditions as preached and practiced by the first leader of the community—the Prophet Muhammad—changed some aspects of these practices but did not abolish all, nor alter Madīna's pre-existing worldview. Among the changes that took place upon the Prophet Muhammad's migration to and settlement in Madīna were the new social divisions he created. He wanted to abolish clan identity and adopt brotherhood among his community.

With Madīna still socially diverse, including members of the Jewish community who were not forced to convert to Islam, the Prophet Muhammad created a new default distinction between believers and nonbelievers. The new distinction meant that believers (who, with the advance of time, would be called Muslims) could not be enslaved, but captives acquired through war were still considered spoils of war, or *ghanā'im*. They were distributed among those eligible, but they could also be traded to free Muslim prisoners held by enemy armies, held and then freed for ransom, or they could buy their own freedom by performing a specialty service such as teaching illiterate Muslims to read and write. Failing that, they could remain slaves indefinitely.[5]

Violence in pre-Islamic Arabia was not just a result of an indigenous culture and its value systems. It was also an adaptation—the direct result of its environment and circumstances, or what we would now call its geopolitical consideration.

---

such, according to some historical records, she was the de facto caliph during the reign of her husband and two sons.

[5] See, generally, Zaydan, *al-Tamaddun al-islāmī*, and 5:39 and 5:139; al-Bayhaqi, *al-Mahasin wa-'l-masawi'*, 613 and 609; and al-Baghdadi, 1:51.

Nowadays, the Middle East is home to violent conflicts and most, if not all, of these conflicts are driven by geopolitical considerations involving parties thousands of miles away. These global actors wish to secure something very valuable to almost everyone's national interest: energy in the form of oil. Most of these wars are proxy wars fought for access to that oil. The same can be said about Mecca and Arabia in the sixth century—the region sat in a location that made it a center of conflict among competing regional and global powers.

The Arabian Peninsula, in the century before Islam and during the first half of the seventh century, was a place of dispute over trade routes involving three empires: Persia in the northeast, Byzantium in the northwest, and Abyssinia in the south. Each of those world powers vied to secure trade routes for their own interests, directly or through proxies. To this end, Abyssinian forces controlled southern Arabia, Yemen and Hadramawt. In 523 CE, for instance, Negus, the Christian king of Abyssinia, sent 60,000 troops to overthrow King Dhu Nuwas. In 570 CE, the year Prophet Muhammad was born, Abraha led a destructive expedition against Mecca; this event, called the Year of the Elephant (*ʿām al-fīl*), was later mentioned in the Quran. When the Persians pushed the Abyssinians back from southern Arabia, and defeated the Abyssinians in 575 CE, they captured and enslaved many African fighters, increasing the number of enslaved Black persons in Arabia to about one-third. The clash of empires around Mecca, the alliances Arab tribes made with the Persians, Byzantines, and Abyssinians, and their participation in wars involving these ethnic groups, was likely the source of slaves of Persian, Byzantine, and Coptic origins in Mecca immediately before the rise of Islam. Therefore, many of the Black and white slaves in Arabia referenced in the Arabic sources were likely enslaved during military conflicts in the second half of the sixth century. Prior to the rise of Islam, enslaved Abyssinians in Mecca were primarily a consequence of war, not part of an international slave trade as would be the case in later centuries.

Before we transition to the Islamic era, or to post-*Jāhiliyya* era as Muslim historians would call it, I should note another aspect of the social and economic structure of Mecca in the sixth century that is relevant to understanding modern Islam and the challenges it faces addressing social problems and questions of legitimacy and institutional governance.

Since Mecca was primarily a trade city-state, inequality must have been a defining feature of society. To establish a trading caravan and build a successful trading business, one needed the capital to invest in the necessary resources and connections. Consequently, to enjoy the property they worked to acquire, Arabs before Islam must have had a commitment to personal property, life, and freedom. They must have established and protected customs, laws, and institutions that enshrined and promoted the right to own property and to freely enjoy it. The flipside of this is that the concentration of wealth must have created more need, resulting in the spread of inequity, poverty, exploitation, classism, and elitism. Importantly, concentration of wealth necessarily leads to concentration of power, which creates power differentials among social groups. Narratives chronicling the birth and rise of Islam reveal that while Quraysh did not have princes and princesses, it had powerful leaders and shrewd businessmen. Sources from pre-Islamic and early Islamic times confirm these conditions, circumstances, and realities.

The most important comparison to make between European societies before and after the Enlightenment and Arab society before and during early Islamic times is their sources of wealth and power. In the 16th and 17th centuries, due to the population decline after famines and plagues, Europe began to shift its economy towards land and capital instead of agriculture. This land ownership-based economy that produced grain and cereals was labor-intensive. In the following centuries, the industrial revolution was also labor intensive. These economic trends created unique dynamics and a special relationship to land, the most enduring and transferrable form of wealth. Landowners' need for labor created rigid social hierarchies and power gradations in societies.

In contrast, in Arabia in the sixth and seventh centuries, the economy was built on the exploitation and consumption of animals and augmentation of wealth though trade. The land, mostly desert and unsuitable for cultivating grains like wheat and barley, was freely used for grazing. Animal husbandry, consisting of raising camels, goats, and sheep, was more important than agriculture. While sheep and goats provided meat and clothing for the family, camels primarily provided transportation and trade. The same way Europeans were attached to their land and estates, Arabs were deeply attached to their camels, about whom poets composed some of the most moving odes. These economic activities were not labor-intensive and were easily managed by unskilled family members. For that reason, families often consisted of one man having multiple sexual relationships—formally through marriage, and informally through concubinage—producing many children who could help herd sheep or trade goods.

In the rest of this introduction, I will tell the story of Islam and the men and women who spread it to create the culture that embraced it; a global civilization that, in a short time, challenged three major empires, and for the first time in recorded history, brought all of the Arabian Peninsula under the rule of one man: Prophet Muhammad. I will provide details useful to gain proper context, and background information necessary to explain significant historical events and institutional developments during Prophet Muhammad's lifetime and after his death that made the modern Islamic world possible.

*****

Born sometime in the second half of the sixth century, Prophet Muhammad came from humble origins. His clan, Banu Hashim, was neither affluent nor influential. From the day he was born and through his young adulthood, he faced adversity and personal loss.

His father, Abdullah, died before he was born. Within his first decade of life, his mother Amina died, leaving him in the care of his paternal grandfather, Abd al-Muttalib, who also died when Prophet Muhammad turned eight. His paternal uncle and the new leader of Bani Hashim, Abu Talib, took him in, and he was raised in the same household as his cousin (and later son-in-law) Ali. When Prophet Muhammad was a baby, he was sent to the countryside (*bādiya*), to live with a female relative who breastfed him, a practice that appears to have been customary for children born in the city. Consequently, his first occupation as a child was as a shepherd. In his late teens, he joined trade caravans connecting Mecca to the Levant region, Shām. His honest management of goods and money for the traders who employed him earned him the moniker *al-Amīn*—the Trustworthy one—which caught the attention of a thrice-widowed, wealthy woman named Khadija. She hired him in his early twenties to manage her trade business. Soon after, Khadija—at this point in her forties—asked him to marry her; he did. Once married, he continued to manage her trading business for another 15 years or so. From this marriage he had all his children: three sons and four daughters; the sons died as infants, but the girls grew up and went on to marry influential members of the community. His daughter Fatima became a central figure in Islamic history, given her place as the mother of the *imams* of Shia Muslims.

Prophet Muhammad's ordinary early life did not predict the extraordinary role he would play in human history. However, many of his social and political positions would, in two decades, transform the Arabian Peninsula and the lives of billions of people. Those accomplishments started when he was in his forties, when he claimed that he was a chosen Messenger sent by God to all of humanity. Despite such an extraordinary claim, Islamic history did not really begin until Prophet Muhammad turned fifty and migrated from Mecca to Madīna.

Prophet Muhammad's claim to divine connections began when he lived in Mecca. At the age of 40, following one of his usual reflective experiences, isolating himself in a cave on a mountaintop overlooking Mecca, he returned home frightened and shaken. He told Khadija about an encounter with a strange being who spoke words to him and ordered him to recite them. It took weeks before he articulated his role and function as the chosen Messenger—*Rasūl*. These encounters, where new words were taught to him (revealed, according to Muslim scholars), would occur again and again until his death. Muslims believe that through these encounters Prophet Muhammad received divine revelations, words, and fragments of recited speech. He taught these words to his followers as the words of God, called the Quran, the Recited Word. After his death, Muslim scholars recorded all of his sayings and deeds, claiming that they too were a form of divine inspiration, just of a lower degree of authority compared to the Quran. Together, the words of the Quran as recited by Prophet Muhammad, and the narratives associated with his life, became the two primary sources of Islamic teachings and practices that Muslims have adhered to ever since. I will discuss the technical aspects of these texts and narratives later in this chapter.

For ten years, Prophet Muhammad—now addressed by his followers as the Messenger or Prophet (*Rasūl; Nabiyy*), or both—preached in Mecca. There he recited the verses of the Quran and interpreted them to nudge Meccans to change their ways, mainly on moral, ethical, and theological matters. He preached that there was no god but the one God, and that he, Prophet Muhammad, was a Messenger from *the* God, Allah. He counseled people to honor and be kind to their parents, to respect the poor and destitute, and to spend their hoarded gold and silver to help the poor and needy. After nearly ten years of preaching this message, only an estimated 300 people joined his movement, and most of them were former slaves, laborers, women, and transient travelers. Only five followers were among the tribal elite, including two key figures, Abu Bakr and `Umar. Nonetheless, Prophet Muhammad's persistence grew in the threat it posed to Quraysh, the governing authority in the city-state, pushing its leaders to issue a sweeping boycott against Prophet Muhammad and his followers: No one was allowed to engage in any transaction with them, and whoever violated this sanction would be subject to the same boycott. Meanwhile, the Prophet Muhammad was already in negotiations with leaders from a city called Yathrib, some 300 miles north of Mecca. Yathrib's leaders, interested in the Prophet's skills as a political leader and mediator, offered him a leadership position in their city. He insisted that he be recognized as a religious leader, a Messenger of God, before accepting their offer. After some negotiation, the leaders of Yathrib agreed to his terms, and on July 16, 622 CE, the Prophet Muhammad and Abu Bakr reached the city of Yathrib, which changed its name to become *al-Madina al-Munawwara*—the City of the Messenger of God—later shortened to simply Madīna: the City.

Upon his arrival in Madīna, the Prophet Muhammad established the first mosque, where Muslims performed their mandatory daily prayers; attached to it was a room for his private residence. He also dictated the terms of a treaty for governing the city-state. Interestingly, while the first institution, *masjid* (mosque), was a place of worship, the second institution—the treaty of Madīna—was a purely secular civil document. The document laid out guidelines for living in a pluralistic city-state where non-Muslims, including Jews, could live according to their own traditions but still honor the terms of the larger community by not aiding or conspiring with outsiders. This kind of pragmatism reflected the skills and abilities that enabled the Prophet to bring all of the Arabian Peninsula under his rule in fewer than 12 years. Before his death, he bequeathed to his successors a stable and prosperous community whose frontiers abutted present-day Iran, Iraq, Byzantium, Jordan, Egypt, Abyssinia, and across the Red Sea. In addition to this vast territory, he also left key institutions and practices that guided his successors to expand their reach.

By the time the Prophet Muhammad died, the Quran had become a source of knowledge, inspiration, and social control. People read it, memorized it, and lived by it. In it, people found ethical and moral guidance as well as legal commands and obligations.

Muslims of that time, just like Muslims today, considered the Quran's explicit teachings as obligations. Where the Quran is implicit, vague, or silent, Muslims referred to the example of the Prophet Muhammad, which, with time, gained the technical name Sunna, or *Hadith*. In fact, `Umar invoked the Sunna, though not by name, to exclude the people of Madīna from seeking the position of caliph; this position, according to `Umar, was a task or an obligation which the people of Quraysh were expected to handle. That first instance of invoking the Sunna/*Ḥadīth* became a powerful precedent, which allowed Muslim leaders and Muslim scholars ever since to draw on the anecdotes of the thoughts and deeds of the Prophet Muhammad, or his key disciples (Companions; *Ṣaḥāba*), to support a legal opinion, an ethical norm, or a political decision. In short, `Umar's action established the Sunna as canonical Islamic law.

Hours after Prophet Muhammad's death of natural causes, during a private meeting in the home of one of Madīna's leaders (*anṣār*), a leadership circle endorsed Abu Bakr to be Prophet Muhammad's successor as a political leader, not as the Prophet. This event set the groundwork for the governing institutions and practices that would inform Islamic political theory and practices for hundreds of years. Generally, Islamic political history can be segmented into four eras, each born out of a violent transformation that tested the community's fidelity to the values enshrined in its religious traditions.

What Muslim historians named the Rashid Caliphate spanned from after the Prophet Muhammad's death through the death of the fourth caliph, Ali, in 661 CE. During this period, Muslim leaders struggled to resolve political, social, and economic problems including cronyism, nepotism, mismanagement of public funds, and social and economic inequity. These challenges resulted in an armed rebellion, which `Aisha, the widow of the Prophet Muhammad, led; and a brutal, protracted civil war—the first of others to follow—that cost thousands of lives including that of the third caliph, `Uthman, who was killed by rebels accusing him of violating the Quranic principles of justice (*`adāla*). The crises of this era revealed Muslim leaders' failure to deal with political dissent.[6] Because of this failure, marginalized and disempowered social groups rebelled. The government failed to repair the damage, which resulted in the first split along sectarian lines and gave birth to Ibadism, the first social movement that has continuously existed since the seventh century.

During this era, the location, procedure, and level of community participation in deliberating over and choosing their political leaders created a culture of exclusion and elitism that marginalized many social groups simply because of their ethnic and economic statuses.

First, because the first meeting to debate succession took place in a private home, *saqīfat bani ṣā`ida*, the majority of Madīna's residents did not take part, especially women and men outside of the elite. Consequently, no woman has ever formally held the central caliphate position in the history of Islamic civilization. The only exceptions of women rising to political rule happened in distant autonomous regions such as the Fatimid dynasty in Egypt and autonomous Berber regions in North Africa.

Second, when `Umar relayed that the Prophet said his successor should be a member of Quraysh, he set a precedent: Everyone who was not both Arab *and* a member of Quraysh was disqualified for the important political leadership position of caliphate. Predictably, all Umayyad and Abbasid caliphs were Arabs and descendants of the tribe of Quraysh, although some Abbasid caliphs might have been only half-Arabs, since some were born to caliphs from

---

[6] Dissenters, especially social groups expressing dissent who were not connected to the ruling elite, were labeled as outsiders, *khawārij*. When `Aisha, the widow of the Prophet and daughter of the first caliph, led an armed rebellion against the fourth caliph, she and her followers were not considered *khawārij*. Those unattached to the ruling elite who asked for fairer distribution of resources were labeled so and pursued militarily. See, generally, Ahmed E. Souaiaia. *Anatomy of Dissent in Islamic Societies: Ibadism, Rebellion, and Legitimacy* (New York: Palgrave Macmillan, 2013).

non-Arab mothers including Berber, Persian, and Byzantine women.[7] As caliph, `Umar took additional actions that strengthened Arab supremacy, although his intent may have been otherwise. For instance, under `Umar's rule, Arab armies that conquered distant territories were not allowed to buy homes or live in those distant cities. He did not want victorious Arabs to take the homes, properties, and places of worship of the people they defeated. Instead, he ordered those wanting to stay to build garrison towns and outposts outside of established cities, so that they would not encroach on the lives of the locals. Many of these garrison towns later became major urban centers, including al-Fusṭāṭ (*al-Fostat*) in Egypt, founded in 641 CE.

Third, due to this precedent, the process of transitioning political leadership became privatized, decided by the reigning caliph before his death through will and bequest, or by a ruling from a select group of advisors often called the People Who Bind and Unbind (*Ahl al-ḥall wa-'l-`aqd*) or the Consultative Council (*Majlis al-shūra*). This group of individuals, generally men from the elite class, would privately nominate and endorse (*bay`a khāṣṣa*) a person. Only after private endorsement would the nominee stand for a general public referendum (*bay`a `āmma*). In fact, even this limited process became obsolete when the caliphate became an inherited institution or position at the start of the Umayyad rule through the Ottoman sultans. Arguably, the precedent the first two caliphs established during this period was what authorized Umayyad and Abbasid rulers to appoint their successors: If it was good for the righteously guided caliphs, these rulers reasoned, it must be good for them.

The Rashid Caliphate era is the only era during which three different caliphs, from four different clans and unrelated by blood, governed and were succeeded by someone unrelated to them. During all other governing eras (the Umayyad, Abbasid, and Ottoman

[7] According to Islamic historical accounts, only three out of 37 Abbasid caliphs were born to free mothers: al-Saffah (d. 136/754), al-Mahdi (d. 169/786), and al-Amin (d. 198/813). All others were born to former slave girls (*jawari*). Cross references were derived from Ibn al-Jawzi's *al-Muntazam* and Ya`qubi's *al-Buldan*.

eras), leadership passed from one person to another within the same family (father-son, father-brother, or brother-brother) or within the same clan. In other words, the caliphate was privatized. One had to belong to a specific clan or ethnic group to be considered for the high political office.

The transition from the Rashid Caliphate to the Umayyad Caliphate took place in the heat of battle and in the context of civil war. Members of the Umayyad clan used calls for revenge for `Uthman's death—at the hands of rebels from as far away as Yemen and Iraq—to challenge `Ali, a Hashimite. The resulting tragic and costly war ended when Caliph `Ali was killed; his son, Hassan, succeeded him but within months offered to settle with his rival Mu`āwiyya, the governor of the Levant, in return for peace and security. Mu`āwiyya, the son of the last chief of Quraysh and ruler of Mecca before it was taken by the Muslims of Madīna, Abu Sufyan, accepted, founding the Umayyad dynastic rule.

From 661 CE to 750 CE, most lands controlled by Muslims fell under the control of the Umayyad clan, the leading force within the tribe of Quraysh before Muslims took control of Mecca. Except for one ruler, Umayyad caliphs were not religious and did not care to appear religious or pious. In fact, Mu`āwiyya's descendants made a habit of offending religious leaders and religious institutions. According to some reports, one used a copy of the Quran as a shooting target and another paraded through the streets of Damascus after soaking his head with wine.[8] The Umayyad rulers' characters, temperaments, and practices transformed the community, institutions, and society in profound ways.

First, the rulers' lack of religious piety, and their appreciation for knowledge, created a path for independent scholars to fill a void that the caliph had traditionally occupied. For the first time, without the Prophet or a caliph spearheading political and religious

[8] Justin Marozzi, *Islamic Empires: Fifteen Cities that Define a Civilization* (UK: Penguin, 2019), 36.

decrees, Muslims had to obey two separate powers: political rulers and religious learned men. In a way, these circumstances secularized Muslim society by separating religious and political authorities. During the lifetime of the Prophet Muhammad, Muslims followed him because he told them that God, the Legislator, revealed the proper law to him. The Prophet Muhammad was the judge and executive. During the reign of the Rashid caliphs, the rulers relied on their recollections of precedents set by the Prophet, the Sunna, to interpret and apply God's rule (*ḥukm*) in society. Under the Umayyads, the *`ulamā'*— the learned ones (*ahl al-`ilm*)—interpreted the Quran and the Sunna for the people. The caliph adopted the *`ulamā's* recommendations. However, the caliphs appointed a learned person to a position in the bureaucracy. These palace scholars, as some circles knew them, had to compete against independent *`ulamā'* for their standing. Independent scholars generally stood out for their piety and, importantly, for their willingness to rise up or endorse uprisings against unjust caliphs and governors.

With the start of the Umayyad rule and through the Abbasid rule, scholars consistently showed their independence by taking part in or endorsing armed rebellion. For instance, the armed "Rebellion of Scholars" marked the first organized armed opposition to the Umayyads and consisted primarily of religious scholars. They fought in a series of battles that ended in 83 AH.

Abu Hanifa, the founder of one of the main Sunni schools of jurisprudence, supported the Zaydi rebellion against Umayyad Caliph Hisham Ibn Abdul Malik, in which Zayd Ibn Ali Ibn al-Hussain Ibn Ali rose up in 122 AH. He framed his rebellion as fighting to follow the book of God and the practices of the Messenger, to fight against oppressors, to protect the oppressed and disempowered, and to return the rights of the exploited.

Malik Ibn Anas (d. 179 AH) also supported another armed uprising, this one led by al-Nafs al-Zakiyya (Muhammad Ibn Abdullah Ibn Hassan Ibn al-Hassan Ibn Ali) against Abbasid Caliph al-Mansur. Malik was arrested, imprisoned, and tortured for this.

Lastly, al-Shafi`i (d. 204 AH), also was imprisoned by Abbasid Caliph al-Rashid for refusing to condemn armed rebellion against rulers.[9]

The divestment of religious authority is the most significant development during this era because it produced an independent institution, the *`ulamā'*, that future political leaders were never able to fully bring back under their direct control. While rulers had their own scholars and judges as part of their bureaucracy, independent scholars continued to exist, and people often trusted them with religious matters over scholars associated with the caliph.

Information about *`ulamā''s* action to preserve the independence of their institution and their rejection of wages and grants from political rulers is chronicled in a number of sources.[10] To preserve their independence, scholars often engaged in trade to make a living; when they were criticized for this, they justified it by claiming that "if it were not for these *dinars* from trade, scholars would have been used by kings and emirs. When you see a scholar seeking the company of caliphs (sultans), know that they are thieves; if they seek the company of the rich, know that they are pretenders; they claim that they are doing what they are doing to help the poor; it is the devil's trick used by some scholars as a ladder to riches."[11] In addition to trade, scholars engaged in manual vocations like carpentry, artisanry, tannery, and jewelry, among other lines of work.[12] Public trust (*waqf*) also played a major role in fostering the

---

[9] See, generally, Thahbi's *Syar a`lām al-nubalā'*; Ibn al-Athir's *al-Kamil*.

[10] See *Ihyā' `ulum al-din* (Ghazzali (d. 505 AH), *al-Dhakhira fi mahasin ahl al-jazira* (al-Shantiri al-Andalusi, d. 542 AH), *Siyar a`lam al-Nubala* and *Tarikh al-Islam* (Dhahbi, d. 748 AH), *Tabaqat al-shafi`iyya* (Sabki, d. 771 AH), *Kifayat al-akhyar fi hal ghayat al-ikhtisar* (Taqiyy al-Din al-Hasni, d. 829 AH), *al-Durra al-gharra' fi nasihat al-slatin wa-'l-quda wa-'l-umara'* (Mahmud Ibn Isma`il al-Khayrabayti, d. 843 AH), *Mā rawāh al-asadin fi `adam al-maji' ila al-sālatin* (Jalal al-Din al-Sayyuti, d. 911 AH), *al-Farq bayna al-firaq* (Abdul al-Qahir al-Baghdad, d. 429 AH).

[11] See *Hilyat al-awliya* (Ahmad Ibn Abdullah al-Asbahani) (d. 430 AH).

[12] For more on the occupations of scholars, see *al-Ansab* (Abu Sa`d al-Sam`ani al-Maruzi, d. 562 AH) and *al-Sunna` min al-fiquha' wa-'l-muhaddithin* (Muhammad Ibn Ishaq al-Sa`di al-Harawi).

independence of educational and learning institutions in Islamic societies. Some of the longest and continuously-operating learning institutions are Islamic *waqf* universities, like al-Qarawiyyin University, founded in 859 CE in Fez, Morocco.[13]

To replace their lost religious authority, the Umayyads emphasized the bonds that connected clans and ethnic identities to secure loyalty and patronage. Members of the Umayyad clan held key positions within bureaucratic and military leadership. Being Arab earned favorable treatment. This strategy stratified society and created new paths for discrimination. Such social engineering practices designated specific social groups as enemies, disloyal subjects, foreigners, or other social labels that bore economic and social consequences.

Such a government is neither just nor inclusive. People often voiced their disapproval, but the government dealt harshly with public dissent. Indeed, immediately after the death of the founder of the Umayyad dynasty and the rise to power of his son, Yazid I, a second brutal civil war broke out, which Muslim historians called *al-Fitna al-thaniya* (the Second Strife), lasting from 780 to 992 CE. Unable to secure uncoerced endorsements from all clan leaders, Yazid sent his security forces to bring them to his palace and required them to publicly pledge an oath of allegiance. The grandson of the Prophet Muhammad, Hussain, refused to endorse Yazid, judging him unjust and therefore illegitimate. He opted to leave for Iraq with about seventy members of his family and supporters. Upon hearing of their travels, however, Yazid sent an army to retrieve Hussain dead or alive. This confrontation resulted in what modern standards would qualify as genocide. Yazid's order

[13] See *Ihya' `ulum al-din* (Ghazzali (d. 505 AH), *al-Dhakhira fi mahasin ahl al-jazira* (al-Shantiri al-Andalusi, d. 542 AH), *Siyar a`lam al-nubala* and *Tarikh al-Islam* (Dhahbi, d. 748 AH), *Tabaqat al-shafi`iyya* (Sabki, d. 771 AH), *Kifayat al-akhyar fi hal ghayat al-ikhtisar* (Taqiyy al-Din al-Hasni, d. 829 AH), *al-Durra al-gharra' fi nasihat al-slatin wa-'l-quda wa-'l-umara'* (Mahmud Ibn Isma`il al-Khayrabayti, d. 843 AH), *Ma rawah al-asadin fi `adam al-maji' ila al-slatin* (Jalal al-Din al-Sayyuti, d. 911 AH), *al-Farq bayna al-firaq* (Abdul al-Qahir al-Baghdad, d. 429 AH).

essentially authorized the destruction of a single social group—the household of Ali's last living son—and the only living grandson of the Prophet Muhammad.

It is impossible to overstate the significance of this event given its implications, execution, and consequences. First, if the head of a government was willing and able to kill and desecrate[14] the grandson of the civilization's founder, what would prevent him from killing other, less significant, dissenters? Second, for a government to allocate that many resources—5,000 troops—to besiege a traveling crowd of 70 people including men, women and children signals the intent to commit a war crime. These two points help explain the third point related to the consequences of this event: Yazid's intent and execution of cruel acts was so traumatizing that it caused the community to convulse and fragment. This event splintered the community and gave birth to the Shia community, who would remember and commemorate the event every year, sacralizing the first ten days of the month of Muharram, reliving the siege and martyrdom of a person who refused to endorse a tyrant. It is often stated in secondary sources that the Shia split occurred immediately after death of the Prophet Muhammad. A close reading debunks that myth. It is true that disagreement occurred early on. But since Ali remained attached to the ruling class, becoming a caliph himself, it would be a mistake to think that Shia, as a distinctive sect and movement, was born at this time. The seeds for splitting may be connected to this time period, but it was only after the brutal killing of Hussain that we can see the formal emergence of a distinctive school of thought and political movement we can call Shia. This moment of violence and strife, like the one during the first *firtna* that resulted in the death of the third caliph, `Uthman, created a second sect in Islam, which has endured ever since. In the context of this work on human rights, while these events signify a religious rite for specific social groups, for the general public they memorialize an instance of human rights abuses at the hands of a government. In ordinary history-making, it might be called a *fitna*

---

[14] Yazid ordered the head of Hussain displayed at one of the gates of Damascus.

(strife) or even romanticized it as a civil war. However, in the context of human rights and humanitarian laws, it must be recognized for what it was: a human rights crime and an act of cruelty that no provocation could justify. Because this event, the tragedy of Karbala, is relived and commemorated yearly across the Islamic world, Muslim thinkers must address it and reflect on it not only in sectarian terms, but also in human rights terms.

Although twelve other Umayyad rulers reigned for over sixty-five years since this event, Muslims could not forget the cruelty inflicted in Karbala. Indeed, half a century after the Karbala massacre, another genocide took place within the Muslim community, but it cannot be explained without returning to and referencing Karbala.

The Umayyad dynasty came to an end when members of the Hashimite clan started an underground opposition movement that swore to remediate the grievances of *Ahl al-Bayt*. Once the Umayyad caliph, Marwan II, learned of the movement, he struck as his predecessors had. Marwan II ordered the capture and cruel killing of the leader of the Abbasid clan, Ibrahim. That action only amplified the anger against the Umayyads, and increased empathy and support for the Hashimite clan. In 750 CE, the younger brother of Ibrahim, Abu Abbas, seized the moment and confronted the Umayyad caliph militarily in a battle near the Zab. Defeated, Marwan II retreated to Egypt to rebuild his army, and Abu Abbas was declared caliph in Kufa and assumed his functions quickly, mobilizing his troops and rushing them to Central Asia to halt an intrusion of the Chinese Tang Dynasty. After he defeated the Chinese in the battle of Talas in 751 CE, he turned his attention to exact his vengeance on the Umayyads, ordering all Umayyad males killed. Essentially, Abu Abbas ordered and executed the second genocide in Islam, killing all male persons belonging to the Umayyad clan, except for a young boy named Abd al-Rahman, who escaped via North Africa and settled in Spain. Abu Abbas crushed any serious threat with an exacting cruelty, earning himself the title of *al-Saffāḥ*, the Blood Spiller. Thirty-six other descendants of al-Abbas went on to rule over most Islamic lands, save the autonomous regions in the peripheries, each one of them taking over the reign of government not because they were the most qualified or as the result of a public mandate, but simply because of who they were in relation to the caliph who preceded them. Success and failure, peace and war, and poverty and prosperity were determined by a caliph's whim, temperament, and character, not by an enduring bureaucracy.

For 508 years, Muslims ruled over most of West Asia and North Africa through the institution of the caliphate, over which a man connected to the Hashimite clan presided. In contrast, the Abbasids ruled over an era of prosperity, security, and progress; however, this progress, security, and prosperity came at a significant human and environmental cost. During the Abbasid rule, while progress occurred in the arts, literature, sciences, and technology, many people became disconnected, exploited, and commodified. Thievery became a way of life, out of contempt for the rich and in sympathy with the poor.[15] Rebellion, like the Revolution of the Blacks (*Thawrat al-zanj*) was common due to exploitation and inequity,[16] as was armed rebellion that championed the cause of farmers exploited by landowners.[17] The caliph established financial institutions and guaranteed financial instruments like banknotes and

---

[15] Muslim historians reference a social movement they called *Lusus*, *Shuttar*, and *`Ayyarun* (thieves, hustlers...) that appeared in Basra and Baghdad in the second and third Islamic centuries during the Abbasid rule, which stole from the rich and gave to the poor. They grew popular and strong, at some point consisting of an army of more than 100,000 troops. This movement was focused on protesting extreme poverty and extreme wealth, and took up arms to work against the extreme inequity. See al-Tabari's *Tarikh al-rusul wa-'l-muluk*, 3:872, 882, 889, 900, 1552, 1566, 1587; al-Mas`udi's *Muruj al-dhahab*, 6:446, 468, and 470.

[16] The armed "Rebellion of the Blacks" was a long struggle that lasted more than fifteen years (255-270 AH/769-883 CE). It involved thousands of people enslaved from east Africa and employed in harsh conditions without meaningful compensation. See al-Tabari's *Tarikh al-rusul wa-'l-muluk*, 3:1745-1773.

[17] See the Qaramite Rebellion, 261-282 AH/874-899 CE, as described by Muslim historians, Ibn al-Athir, 7:137 and al-Tabari, 3:2130; this movement, based on their teachings, is seen as the first communist movement that accused religious figures, including Muhammad and Jesus, of tricking the people with promises of salvation in another world while enslaving them in this world through religious dogma. See, al-Baghdadi's *Tarikh baghdad*, 281-88.

currencies, allowing wealthy Muslims to travel the world for trade and pleasure. In short, during the Abbasid rule, Muslims became the engine of a civilization stretching from Mauritania to Mongolia. With success, however, comes failure and abuse. By the middle of the thirteenth century, the Abbasid caliphate was overcome with the effects of its own laxity and glut and was overrun by the Mongols. In the span of about ten years, power gradually jumped for the first time from the Hashimite clan into the hands of non-Arabs. People of Turkic descent rose to power, moving up the ranks of a powerful military and eventually moving the seat of the caliphate to Anatolia, signaling the rise of the Ottoman Empire, also called the Ottoman Sultanate.

The Ottoman Empire was, in a way, an inevitable outcome of a civilization that amassed too much wealth and ignored the needs of too many of its subjects. Like any empire, the Ottoman Sultanate focused on building military and administrative institutions that allowed it expansion and control. Coercion—rather than persuasion or collaboration—became the mode of control. Indigenous communities were forced to assimilate and change how they lived. Previously, caliphs often appointed locals who converted to Islam to rule over their communities. The Ottomans, however, preferred to dispatch a Turkish *bey* or *dey* to govern over indigenous communities. Abuse of power, previously familiar to Muslims of different sects within Islamic societies, became the experience of other faiths. The Armenian genocide is just one example of an outcome of empire rule. All the abuses and the emphasis on military power only increased resentment and lack of faith in a government too distant to connect with local peoples. By the eighteenth century, many Muslims favored European colonial powers over Ottoman rule, leading to the latter's disintegration and shrinking, and opening the door for colonial powers to fill the vacuum and start their own expansion and occupation of Muslim-majority regions.

The above introduction preserves the division of the Islamic civilization into key eras or dynasties, a timeline Khallāf used to trace the origins and development of important events, ideas, and institutions. This overview should provide a holistic view of Islamic civilization in general and enable the reader to engage with Khallaf's account of Islamic law and governance institutions.

In this introduction, due to vocational bias, a point of emphasis anchors the account: the state of rights in Islamic society before the colonial period. Furthermore, this introduction highlights rights abuses more than references to rights abuses appear in Khallaf's translated work; that is driven by at least several considerations. First it is the outcome of professional bias. Second, it is an attempt at balancing, to account for Khallaf's lack of engagement with the issue of rights, both in this work and in all his other works. Third, such an introduction tethers the Islamic institutions of the classical period to the one of the ever-present issues of modern Western civilization. Lastly, an emphasis on rights, and more specifically on rights abuses in Islamic civilization, is intended to underscore the fact that human rights abuses are universal—not justified, but universal—and the universal perpetrator of rights abuses is the State (or the government, before the "State" was adopted as a legal person).

Human rights abuses are crimes the State commits against specific social groups. This does not mean that crimes social groups commit against one another are not human rights crimes. However, even those crimes should be seen as government crimes, since governments allow such crimes to happen or do not bring to justice those responsible. Therefore, all governments are guilty of human rights crimes. Importantly, another government or an international organization would not need to characterize these actions as rights offenses. Often the abuse is a violation of the laws and policies the government itself recognizes and uses to legitimize itself. For example, when some Muslims rebelled during the rule of the third caliph, `Uthman, these people believed that the caliph's actions were abusive based on the teachings of the Quran, to which `Uthman had sworn to adhere. When Hussain and others refused to endorse Yazid's rule, they invoked the same principles, values, and rules within Islamic traditions and institutions that judged him to be abusive. Every other instance of dissent and rebellion within Islamic societies throughout the history of Islamic civilization points to the government's abuse of power based on the standards that it swore to uphold. With these facts in mind, it is essential to understand the nature and functions of the Islamic caliphate and the governing, legal, and judicial institutions and practices that rendered it legitimate.

Many modern thinkers, both Muslim and non-Muslim, argue that Islam's problem is with its inability to become secular. They often argue that the interconnectedness of Islamic religious and political discourse makes any Islamic government a form of theocracy and, as such, incompatible with human rights norms. This view is false when we look at the data. The caliphate is different from the modern State in that the caliph is the sovereign but not the institution. It follows, then, that the majority of Islamic governments (caliphs) were more secular than theocratic.[18] Timewise, Muslims have lived under secular governments for far longer than they have lived under the rule of a government that one could call a theocracy. This is true even using a very loose definition of "theocracy," which normally refers to a system of government where a religious authority such as an *imām* rules in the name of God.

In the pan-Islamic caliphate, Sunnism was the official sect to which rulers ostensibly adhered. In Sunnism, there is no infallible religious person who acts as an intermediary between God and the people. Learned persons qualify as religious scholars, all of whom are equal. The only event that could elevate the status of one scholar (or school of thought) over another is the government adopting it as official. Islamic dynasties and caliphs often did so: Most Ottoman Sultans embraced Hanafism as the official school of jurisprudence; the Islamic Emirate in Spain adopted Malikism at one

[18] Most readers today might assume that the caliphate was a "legal person," similar to our modern State. However, in the Islamic system, the caliphate was an institution that had no legal standing as a legal person. The caliph, meanwhile, was a legal person, and it was the caliph's character that gave the government its nature as either religious or secular.

time and Zahirism at another as official schools of jurisprudence; and, most recently, Saudi Arabia adopted Wahhabist-interpreted Salafism as the privileged school of jurisprudence and theology. Short of such action by the State, any learned person could be considered a religious authority. However, the same was not true for all caliphs. Even if we consider piety to be a form of religious authority, not actual knowledge, most caliphs would not qualify as pious.

Despite all the emphasis on just rule and righteous government, Muslims have been ruled by corrupt and cruel leaders far longer than they have been under righteous leaders. Specifically, since the death of the Prophet and until the formal disintegration of the Ottoman Empire, Muslims lived under 98 caliphs and sultans (excluding autonomous regions). Only six of these met the conditions of a just leader according to Muslim legal scholars. In other words, fewer than 6% of leaders were just, which means that 94% of them have abused the human rights of one social group or another. This underscores the fact that governments, taken as a whole, are abusers of human rights or potential abusers of human rights. A plan to universalize human rights must take into consideration these hard facts.

Timewise, the caliphate and sultanate rule covered 1,292 years, with no more than 55 of those years under righteous rule. It would appear that righteous rule is the exception, not the norm, under the Islamic caliphate system.

Developing a human rights-centered action plan must account for that statistic: What must be done when—not if—governments violate and abuse rights? The answer cannot be to simply create a better government. It must be to create a counterbalance to government power, in order to discourage the State from committing rights abuses and hold the State accountable when it does.

Considering that human rights are essentially a balance between social groups' rights and government overreach, we must consider the institutions of Islam that have the most impact on human rights claims—that is, the people entitled to be caliphs, and the function of the caliph as government.

Muslim religious scholars see the caliph as an executive entrusted with applying the guidelines and rules of Sharia among Muslims to realize justice.[19] This brief definition connects all the foundational elements of the theories of governance in Islam. It identifies the caliph as an executive, not a legislator; Sharia as the source of law; and the goal of Sharia as realizing divine justice. Muslims scholars developed a list of qualifications required for the job of caliph, some more detailed than others. Summarizing a view held by most Sunni scholars, an eleventh century Shafi`i jurist argued that for one to qualify to be a caliph, one must meet seven conditions:[20]

1. Probity (*`adāla jāmi`a*)
2. Knowledge (*`ilm*)
3. Ability to discern (*salāmat al-hawāss*)
4. Physical abilities (*salāmat al-'a`ḍā'*)
5. Wisdom (*al-ra'y al-mufḍi*)
6. Courage (*al-shajḍ`a*)
7. Lineage (*nasab, quraysh*)

The fourteenth century Islamic scholar Sad al-Din Mas`ud Ibn Umar Ibn Abd Allah al-Taftazani, on the other hand, adds being male (*dhukūra*) and being free (not enslaved) as conditions for one to hold the position of caliph.[21]

---

[19] See Abd al-Razzaq Ahmed al-Sanhuri, *Fiqh al-khilafa* (Cairo: Muassasat al-risala, 2008), 79.

[20] Al-Mawardi (Abu al-Hassan Ali Ibn Habib al-Basri), *al-Ahkam al-sultaniya* (Cairo: Dar al-Hadith, 2006), 20.

[21] Taftazani explains that *al-nisa' naqisat aql wa-din mamnu`at mina al-khuruj ila al-mashahi wa-mughawarat al-hurib*. See, al-Taftazani, *Taqrib al-maram* (Beirut: Dar al-Kutub al-Ilmiya, 2017), 356.

The idea that the caliph, who since Umayyad times has inherited a powerful position for no other reason than his affinity to the previous caliph, is bound by the terms of another institution, Sharia, is easy to dismiss as pure fiction. It might be, since statistically the majority of the caliphs and sultans do not meet most of the conditions established by the *'ulamā'*. The dissonance between reality and theory brings the logical question: Why is it important to invoke Sharia when it has failed to limit the transgressions of caliphs in the past, and is seen today as a primary force behind human rights abuses?

What is Sharia?

The Ottoman Sultanate, which governed over most geographical regions where Muslims were a majority, was the last pan-Islamic political order. With its fall, Sharia gained new meanings and functions in Islamic societies and beyond. By the start of the twenty-first century, Sharia was invoked to contextualize cultural, geopolitical, and religious conflicts. The 2011 protest movements and wars ushered in radical changes, which made Sharia a central topic of debate wherever Muslims existed in significant numbers.

In Muslim-majority countries, where leaders debate and negotiate legal reforms, the persistent question is whether Sharia should be *the* source of law or *a* source of law. In countries where Muslims are minorities, some local and national governments have proposed laws banning the adoption of Sharia.[22] In territories and countries controlled by Islamist armed groups, Sharia courts have been established and self-styled scholars have imposed themselves as chief Sharia judges (sing. *qāḍī shar'ī*). Social movements, violent

[22] See, generally, Anna C. Korteweg and Jennifer A. Selby, eds., *Debating Sharia: Islam, Gender Politics, and Family Law Arbitration* (Toronto: University of Toronto Press, 2012).

and non-violent, have emerged in many Muslim-majority countries with activists demanding the "implementation of Sharia" in their communities.

These events might give the impression that Sharia is a concrete and well-defined concept, body of law, and legal system. In reality, Sharia—while anyone can invoke it —cannot be found on the bookshelves of libraries and bookstores, in digital archives, or in any other singular standardized storing mechanism. Indeed, there is no consensus, especially among Muslim religious scholars, let alone among scholars specializing in the critical study of Islam, on the meaning and functions of Sharia.[23] However, texts from Islam's formative period, especially during times of dissent and rebellion, provide a glimpse into that generation's understanding of Sharia and its functions in a society. Analyzing this evidence, through lingo-cultural, logical, and teleological lenses, helps reconstruct the social forces that built Islamic civilization.

Today, in Western societies, fear of Sharia might be explained in several ways. Prejudice and bigotry drive many people to oppose any idea or action that could mainstream a cultural or religious legacy of an othered community.[24] Established dominant religious communities often work to exclude competing religious expressions. Many people, however, take anti-Sharia and anti-Muslim positions because they do not actually know the meaning and functions of Sharia.[25] Their information about Sharia often comes from

---

[23] A recent work dedicated to answering the question, What is the Sharia?, concluded that Sharia "does not have an intrinsic meaning accessible to, at any rate, human understanding... most classical scholars did not evoke the Sharia and did not claim to know it." Baudouin Dupret, *What is the Sharia?* (Oxford: Oxford University Press, 2018), 7-9.

[24] Dominic McGoldrick, "Accommodating Muslims in Europe: From Adopting Sharia Law to Religiously Based Opt Outs from Generally Applicable Laws," *Human Rights Law Review*, 9, no. 4 (2009): 603–45.

[25] Sarah M. Fallons, "Justice for All: American Muslims, Sharia Law, and Maintaining Comity within American Jurisprudence," *International & Comparative Law Review*, 153 (2013).

reports of harsh punishments in a far-away land under some brutal regime, Sharia the primary culprit.[26]

Recently, Islamist groups seizing control of vast territories and imposing cruel punishments in the name of Sharia law have appropriated and defined Sharia as a concrete legal code of rules and punishments.

It must be noted that some Muslim politicians' inclination to impose Sharia law is not limited to the twenty-first century and is not a result of the 2011 social change movements and wars. In the 20th century, many authoritarian Muslim rulers imposed Sharia law (selectively imposing harsh punishments in the name of Sharia) to acquire legitimacy. In Sudan in September 1983, Jaafar Nimeiri imposed a form of Sharia law throughout the country, amputating the hands of thieves to win support from religious groups. Omar al-Bashir, too, embraced a form of Sharia regime to appease opposition groups and to distract people from the fact that he grabbed power through military coup. In Pakistan, starting in 1977, General Muhammad Zia-ul-Haq took steps to introduce Sharia laws and establish Sharia courts.

Generally, these assumptions, presumptions, and actions have themselves been the primary sources of information about Sharia, since individuals cannot consult a Sharia book themselves; no standard book of Sharia exists. What *is* on the shelves of libraries and bookstores or in digital archives are collections of *fiqh*, which literally means an *understanding* of Sharia. These collections are always tagged according to their scholars' specific sect (*tā`ifah*; *firqah*), or to a particular school of jurisprudence (*madhhab/mazhab*) within their sect. Theological and political disputes have produced three major historical Islamic sects: Sunnism, Ibadism, and Shi`ism. Meanwhile, purely jurisprudential disputes have produced nine schools of jurisprudence within each sect: Within

[26] See, generally, Anna C. Korteweg and Jennifer A. Selby, eds., *Debating Sharia: Islam, Gender Politics, and Family Law Arbitration* (Toronto: University of Toronto Press, 2012).

Sunnism are Malikism, Hanafism, Shafi`ism, and Ḥanbalism; under the umbrella of Shi`ism are Ja`farism, Zaydism, and Isma`ilism; and Ibadism comes in Eastern and Western forms. Theological arguments and disputes fall in a genre called *uṣūl al-dīn*, whereas legal arguments belong to the theoretical genre, *uṣūl al-fiqh*. It is in *fiqh* collections in each school of jurisprudence where one can find the body of law.

Both Muslim religious scholars and Islamicists[27] reference Sharia as if it were a concept, instrument, or institution upon whose meaning there was a universal consensus. Despite its ubiquity, Sharia remains a highly ambiguous term. That ambiguity has led to its sociopolitical use and abuse. In popular non-Arabic narratives, Sharia is often "translated" or explained as Sharia law, the Islamic legal system, Islamic law, religious law, God's immutable divine law, or a faith-based code of conduct.[28] Is Sharia any—or all—of these descriptors? And if so, why not simply use the term "Islamic law" and drop the Arabic word Sharia to avoid confusion and fearmongering? To answer this and related critical questions, it will be helpful to examine the ways both Muslim scholars and Islamicist researchers define and use the word "Sharia."

---

[27] An Islamicist is a secular university-trained scholar of Islamic civilization specializing in classical Islamic thought and institutions. The qualification "secular" distinguishes a scholar *on* Islam from a scholar *of* Islam. A Muslim scholar may attend an Islamic university that teaches traditional disciplines as part of its curriculum to train *imāms*. But such a person would not be one we would label as Islamicist.

[28] For sample definitions of Sharia by Islamicists, see Baudouin Dupret, *What is the Sharia?* (Cambridge: Oxford University Press, 2018), Patricia Sloane-White, *Corporate Islam: Sharia and the Modern Workplace* (Cambridge: Cambridge University Press, 2017), Maurits Berger, ed., *Applying Sharia in the West: Facts, Fears and the Future of Islamic Rules on Family Relations in the West* (Leiden : Leiden University Press 2013), A. Kevin Reinhart, "Islamic Law as Islamic Ethics," *Journal of Religious Ethics*, 11, no. 2 (1983): 186-203, N. Coulson,, "The State and the Individual in Islamic Law," *International and Comparative Law Quarterly* 6 no. 1 (1957): 49-60, Irshad Abdal-Haqq, "Islamic Law - An Overview of Its Origin and Elements," *Islamic Law & Culture* 27 (2002), and Yvonne Yazbeck Haddad and Barbara Freyer Stowasser, *Islamic Law and the Challenges of Modernity* (Lanham, MD: Rowman Altamira, 2004).

Contextualizing Islam in the broader Semitic religious tradition, one could argue that the idea of a Sharia-inspired code, as derived from the Quranic text, is some version of the Ten Commandments. However, this analogy has limits. First, according to Jewish and Christian religious scholars, the Ten Commandments were written on stone tablets, intended as strict rules. Second, the Commandments are commands, appearing in two chapters of the Bible: the Book of Exodus in Chapter 20, and the Book of Deuteronomy in Chapter 5. With the Quran, however, while a few of these Commandments are explicitly stated in the Quran, most are implied, and they appear throughout the Quran rather than concentrated in two chapters. The Quran refers to the tablets but does not list any commandments. If it is the explicitness of rules that determines a religious code's existence (such as Sharia), then textual evidence points more strongly to the existence of a Judeo-Christian Sharia than the existence of an Islamic Sharia.

Considered throughout Islamic history as broad principles guiding lawmaking, Sharia is nebulous because it is derived from Quran texts. The Quran, compared to the Bible, is not a coherent narrative. It is neither a collection of stories nor a clear code of legal injunctions. As far as storytelling is concerned, the Quran depends substantively on Biblical stories for an uninformed reader to make sense of most of its narratives. Not only is the Quran dependent on Jewish and Christian scripture and Rabbinic and Biblical scholars for specific details, but each individual passage of the Quran is dependent on other Quranic passages to contextualize its meaning. Muslim scholars rarely, if ever, use a single passage from the Quran to explain a concept. Instead, they cite numerous passages from the Quran to account for the full range of meanings of a word or a law, and determine the proper context in any given case.

There is something else unique about Islamic Sharia as compared to Judeo-Christian Sharia—to wit, the Commandments. In theory, as a basis of law, a central political order consistently and continuously promulgated and implemented Islamic Sharia for nearly 1300 years. Although no central infallible religious figure analogous to the Pope has existed in Islamic lands, the caliph as a person and the caliphate as an institution made Sharia a living legal code. In fact, these caliphs stood in for the Prophet Muhammad immediately after his death and made it their primary function to implement Sharia, legitimizing them in the eyes of the community. Caliphs, in the eyes of Muslims, are God's agents on earth, charged with the singular task of establishing divine justice.[29] However, every time a caliph was challenged, removed, or delegitimized, as cited earlier in this chapter, his challenger invoked the same claim: He was there to re-establish divine justice as instructed in the Quran and the Sunna. In other words, Sharia was where divine justice resided, as claimed by all—those in power and those opposed to them. Indeed, the implementation of Sharia's principles and rules fell into the hands of the caliphs, but the authority to determine Sharia rule concerning a specific event under specific circumstances rested, most times, with *`ulamā'* (sing. *`ālim*).[30] The determination of who was *`ālim* and who was not was also independent from the caliphs' authority and power.

While there were, as is the case nowadays, some *`ulamā'* who were formally educated and trained in government-run institutions, many *`ulamā'* received private educations, were self-educated, or learned from attending unaffiliated learning courts; these *`ulamā'* became equally authoritative, and perhaps more influential, than government-certified and appointed scholars. Generally, reputation served a stronger role in the status of a religious scholar than formal education. In a sense, the caliph could help establish the status of the *`ulamā'* both ways: He could legitimize those within the establishment through formalities, and could also legitimize those outside the establishment by their opposition to and

[29] Hugh Kennedy, *Caliphate: The History of an Idea* (New York: Basic Books, 2016), 1.

[30] It should be noted that scholars would often, if not always, refer to the opinion (*ra'y*) of the *`ulamā'*, using the plural form of the word, and rarely, if ever, the singular form. This suggests at least two things: *`ulamā'* is more of an institution then a group of scholars, and an individual opinion by a single *`alim* lacks precedential authority until it is independently confirmed by other scholars.

watchfulness of him. The authority and standing of scholars within the establishment, and that of scholars outside the establishment, oscillated depending on the public's view of the caliph. When the caliph lacked public trust and standing as a pious and just leader, such as Yazid Ibn Mu`āwiyya, more people revered and trusted scholars from outside the establishment and appreciated their independence. On the other hand, when a caliph was respected and trusted, such as Umar II, the stock of scholars within the establishment rose, perhaps at the expense of those outside the establishment.

The institution of *`ulamā'* is vital to the meaning and functions of Sharia because it is through *`ulamā'* that Sharia comes alive in society. Some Muslim scholars argue that Sharia is the mathematical absolute sum of individual maxims and principles and the settled determination of learned religious scholars. The whole of the Quran exists in the memories of *`ulamā'* and the example of the Prophet is in their imaginations, allowing *`ulamā'*, at any single moment, to know the Sharia principle that is most appropriate to the case before them.

Other Muslim scholars contend that Sharia is a set of principles and guidelines that scholars use to derive laws and punishments. However, there is no single authoritative text that lists these principles and guidelines. The Quran does not contain a specific section focused on the principles and guidelines of Sharia. Yet some Muslim scholars assert that the Quran is the primary source of Islamic law. The Quranic principles ostensibly foundational to Sharia are embedded within the Quran's moral and ethical stories; they remain open to interpretation.

Defining Sharia and distinguishing among Sharia, *uṣūl*, and *fiqh* are two of the key challenges that both Islamists and Islamicists face.[31] The distinction between Sharia and *fiqh* varies not only

[31] See this sample definition of *fiqh* by Orientalists: "Fiqh is a system of rules and methods whose authors consider it to be the normative interpretation of the revelation, the application of its principles and commands to the field of human acts."

between theological sects and jurisprudential schools of thought, but also from one *`alim* to another within the same school of thought. Scholars of Islamic studies in North American and European educational institutions, too, present radically different explanations of Sharia and *fiqh*. I shall provide a summary of these explanations from classical as well as modern Muslim scholars. The summary will reveal the broad range of opinions and deep disagreement over the definition of Sharia and its related subjects.

Modern Muslim scholars, such as the head of al-Azhar, often qualify something as acceptable or unacceptable in both Sharia and law.[32] This qualification reflects the settled position among Muslim scholars that Sharia *is distinct from law*. Other Muslim scholars contend that Sharia is broader than *fiqh* because of the former's jurisdiction. Sharia rulings, they argue, are those which apply to all people and which are supported by unambiguous legal proof[33] in the primary sources (*naṣṣ*; the Quran and the Ḥadīth/Sunna), and not subject to interpretation. *Fiqh*, on the other hand, is the body of opinions of legal scholars (*faqīh, pl. fuqahā'*) within a specific school of jurisprudence; these opinions may lack legal proof or rely on legal proofs from outside the primary sources. *Fiqh*-based laws are produced through informed legal reasoning called *ijtihād*, which is specific to its historical and geographic circumstances.[34]

Rules and rulings are also key concepts associated with Sharia.[35] The Arabic root, *h-k-m*, refers to halting corruption in something and restoring it to its wholesome state so that it can fulfill the purpose that *fiqh*, sciences (*`ulūm*), and wisdom (*ḥikma*) have determined for it. Therefore, the *hakim* (in the sense of Qadi), halts aggression (*ẓulm*) and establishes justice.[36] For legal scholars, *al-*

Baber Johansen, *Contingency in a Sacred law: Legal and Ethical Norms in Muslim Fiqh* (Leiden: Brill, 1999), 1. See, also, Korteweg, *Debating Sharia*.

32 *shar`an wa-qanunan.*

33 *Dalil.*

34 *al-ijtihād ibnu zamanihi wa-makanih.*

35 *al-hukm al-shar`i.*

36 see, *Lisan al-arab, h-k-m* entry.

ḥukm al-shar`ī refers to the range of rules judging an act as obligatory (*wājib*), recommended (*mandub/mustaḥabb*), permitted (*mubāḥ*), recommended against (*makrūh*), or proscribed (*muḥarram (ḥarām)*). Most know these legal judgments as the five legal rules.[37] For most jurists (*uṣūlis*), however, these are the five legal effects of the legal ruling;[38] for jurists, the legal ruling is the actual text of the Legislator (God) as stated in the Quran and the Sunna.

The Salafist scholar Ibn Taymiyyah proposes yet another distinction between Sharia and *fiqh*. He cites some religious scholars and members of the public who believe that the words "*sharia*" and "*shar`*" apply to acts governed by the science of *fiqh*, and who distinguish between matters of creed (*`aqā'id*) and laws (*sharā'i`*), or truth and law.[39] He further clarifies that:

> Sharia encompasses all matters related to acts of benefit in this world or in the Hereafter. Sharia is the book of God and the Sunna of his Prophet, and that which was the practice of the ancestors (*salaf*) in areas of creed (*`aqa'id*), civil law, worship, and politics.[40]

Echoing the opinion of most Traditionalist[41] scholars, Ibn Taymiyyah argues that the Quran and the Sunna contain answers to all possible questions that human beings, anywhere and anytime, might face:

> The opinion of our ancestral authorities (*salaf*) and the majority of legal scholars (*fuqaha'*) and theologians (*mutakallimin*) is this: God has issued a ruling on every event and for every event God has predetermined a specific ruling, be it obligation, proscription,

---

[37] *al-ahkam al-shar`iyya al-khamsa.*
[38] *al-hukm al-shar`i.*
[39] See Ibn Taymiyyah, *al-Fatawa al-kubra*, 4:231.
[40] Ibid.
[41] I employ the term "Traditionist" in reference to *Ahl al-hadith.*

> permission, or absence of obligation and proscription, which we called allowance (*`afw*). Therefore, no human being can ignore Sharia as it relates to all their dealings, because all that would benefit them is found in Sharia.[42]

According to Ibn Taymiyya, whose works are considered normative in Salafism, Sharia is one and the same as religious teachings. Sharia is, in other words, Islam. Moreover, religious teachings, which he considers sacred and divine, include the consensus (*ijma'*) of the learned ancestors (*salaf*). Sharia, thus defined, is also complete: It contains answers to all possible questions and cases. Lastly, according to Salafism, benefit to human beings is what drives Sharia. However, such benefits are also predetermined in the same source of the law, which is different from Reasonist[43] scholars' understanding of benefit (*maṣlaḥa*). For non-Salafist scholars, people may engage in beneficial activities independent of the sources of law. Sharia laws are intended to preserve those benefits. An example can illustrate this difference. Personal property—private ownership of resources—has some benefits in society in that it creates some social and economic order. Most Muslim religious scholars would argue that Sharia-inspired laws preserve and protect personal property rights. Salafist scholars, on the other hand, would argue that individual property rights are Sharia-mandated as being the only beneficial form of economic order. Any other form of property ownership, in their view, would conflict with the absolute, immutable Sharia rule.

Stressing the linguistic meaning of Sharia as the path to the waterway, some Muslim religious scholars draw the following analogy: The same way the physical wellbeing of a human body is dependent on water, the material and mental welfare of a human is dependent on following Sharia. They stress that Sharia, as such, covers all aspects of life. Explicitly or by way of general rule, Sharia

---

[42] Taymiyyah, *al-Fatawa al-kubra*, 9:307.

[43] "Reasonist" is used to denote the Arabic phrase, *Ahl al-ra`y*.

determines the proper ruling for every possible event a human might face.

Consequently, Muslim religious scholars agree on one idea: Sharia is general, broad, and principle-driven. Those are the characteristics that distinguish Sharia from *fiqh* and related legal disciplines. Specifically, Islamic legal manuals argue that *fiqh* is an informed determination of the proper ruling deriving from the legal proofs. The legal scholar (*faqih*) is charged with deriving legal rulings from Sharia proofs (the Quran and the Sunna) or other sources Sharia empowers, such as consensus (*ijmā`*) and proper analogy (*qiyās ṣaḥīḥ*). The legal scholar, therefore, specializes in deriving legal rulings on practical matters, without involving themselves in matters of creed (*al-umūr al-`aqdiyya*). *Fiqh*, in sum, is the acquired knowledge based on legal proofs (*al-dalīl al-shar`ī*), covering legal rulings on practical matters.[44]

As shown in the above discussion, the definition of Sharia is ever-evolving and subject to an emerging understanding shaped by internal and external pressures. The old boundaries are less isolating, allowing for an adaptive understanding of Sharia. Some modern Muslim religious scholars argue that Sharia consists of two types: a general Sharia covering theological matters, socio-economic transactions, and ethics; and a specific Sharia referring to practical cases not theological or ethical in nature. This understanding essentially explains the difference between the general statements and specific legal rulings, both found in the Quran. This position diverges from another explanation some modern Muslim religious scholars have proposed, arguing that both general and specific rulings belong to Sharia. However, Sharia is the specific rulings stated in the primary sources, whereas the rulings jurists have derived through *ijtihād* from the primary sources belong to *fiqh*. The difference between these two definitions is significant. The first definition conflates *fiqh*, as the body of law, with the legal and ethical principles from the Quran and the Sunna. The second

[44] See al-Amidi, *al-Ihkām fī al-ahkām*, 1:5.

definition establishes a body of law derived from the Quran and the Sunna, constituting Sharia, and a second body of law derived from these primary sources through *ijtihād*, constituting *fiqh*. The explicit laws stated in the Quran are Sharia laws, whereas *ijtihād*-based rulings are called *fiqh* laws.

A third perspective further complicates Muslim scholars' attempts to establish a universal definition of Sharia. Some contemporary Muslims scholars define Sharia as all revealed teachings. That is to say that Sharia is all of the Quran and all teachings of the Prophet Muhammad. *Fiqh*, on the other hand, is the all-encompassing legal discipline that reflects humans' understanding of the religious teachings and consists of jurisprudence (*uṣūl*) and law (*furū`*). This understanding presents Sharia to mean the religion (*al-din*) and *fiqh* as the jurists' understanding of the religion. The domain of Sharia is broad, covering theological, ethical, and practical matters. *Fiqh*, on the other hand, covers only practical matters. In other words, *fiqh* as defined here is not human understanding of the whole; it is part of the whole. *Fiqh* thus conceived is different from *fiqh* defined as the informed judgment of the jurist, regardless of whether their judgment is correct or erroneous.

The imminent Sunni institution al-Azhar provides yet another distinction between Sharia and *fiqh*. According to al-Azhar, Sharia is all the divine teachings as revealed to the Prophet Muhammad. *Fiqh* is the human understanding of these teachings and their application to produce legal norms and legal decrees. Such legal norms and decrees consider not only the legal proofs (*dalīl*) found in the primary sources (the Quran and the Sunna), but consider also the circumstances involving place, time, event, and actors. Having said this, it becomes evident that a direct statement from the Quran, even if it is clear and explicit, is not part of the *fiqh* because, for something to be part of *fiqh*, it must be processed through intellect and contextualized by the specific circumstances.[45] This characterization clarifies that *fiqh* is not and cannot be Sharia, because only Sharia is unbound by time, place, and circumstances—that is, universal.

Notwithstanding the lack of consensus on the relationship between Sharia and *fiqh*, Sunni Muslim religious scholars do agree on Sharia's character. They conclude that Sharia is broad, consisting primarily of general principles. These principles then guide Muslim legal, ethical, and theological scholars in producing the practical and detailed rules in each of these areas. Subsequently, legal scholars produce *fiqh*, and such a *fiqh* is—unlike Sharia—limited. Sharia thus defined is intimately connected to religious texts and traditions, whereas *fiqh*, by definition, is merely humans' understanding of Sharia. Even in places with rulers who adhere to the most conservative interpretations of Islam, like Saudi Arabia,[46] religious scholars tend to equate Sharia to Islam and *fiqh* to law. In the case of Saudi Arabia, members of the cabinet (*majlis al-wuzarāʾ*) endorse law. In this context, *fiqh*, not Sharia, is of two kinds: judgments gleaned from primary sources and judgments derived from religious primary sources through *ijtihād*.[47]

In summary, religious scholars do not distinguish between Sharia and the contents of the Quran and the Sunna. According to the majority of Sunni scholars, there is no distinct body of law called Sharia law because Sharia is more than law. Law, for them, is found in *fiqh* collections, which jurists produce through the process of informed independent reasoning, *ijtihād*.

From this brief overview of Muslim scholars' opinions on the meaning and functions of Sharia and *fiqh*, it is clear that there is no authoritative consensus. However, they agree on this: Sharia is

---

[45] Based on public remarks delivered by an al-Azhar official, Mohammed Kamal al-Din Iman, archived at https://swaana.integr8d.org.
[46] Daryl Champion, *The Paradoxical Kingdom: Saudi Arabia and the Momentum of Reform* (New York: Columbia University Press, 2003).
[47] R. Hrair Dekmejian, "The Rise of Political Islamism in Saudi Arabia," *Middle East Journal* 48, no. 4 (1994): 627-43.

broader in scope than *fiqh;* and Sharia, as provided by the Lawgiver (God), is the source of the principles that guide lawmakers who produce the body of law (*fiqh*). Despite this consensus, Muslim jurists and western experts in Islamic law do not identify a catalog of Sharia principles or a hierarchy of such principles. Each scholar can use a principle from the primary source to justify their ruling on any given case. Some argue that the degree of explicitness and implicitness of a principle's legal proof (*dalīl*), not its nature, decides its potency. In theory, such distinctions seem reasonable. However, they lose all meaning when actual cases present themselves. For example, Sharia ruling on theft (*sariqa*) is well-known to Muslim jurists from all major theological and jurisprudential schools, because the Quran contains an explicit statement respecting the male and female thief.[48] Yet the Quranic text prescribes the punishment for someone who *is* a male or female thief but does not prescribe the punishment for the *act* of theft; there is no explicit definition of theft. Consequently, the definition of theft fell to the jurists and as expected, they did not agree on a single definition. Clearly, the presence of explicit text in a primary source does not establish a class of cases for which Sharia ruling is predetermined. Some Muslim religious scholars' distinctions—between Sharia as a body of law explicitly addressed in the primary sources (Quran and Sunna) and *fiqh* as a body of law derived through *ijtihād*—are unsupported by facts and logic. First, there is no collection of Sharia law that stands independent from *fiqh* collections. Second, even explicit texts of the Quran dealing with transactional legal matters (*mu`āmalāt*) are a subject of deep disagreement among Muslim scholars on aspects including definition, scope, and circumstances.

Indeed, the body of legal and jurisprudential legacy Muslim scholars have produced is complex and diverse, the result of their sectarian and methodological differences. That diversity aside, the majority of Muslim scholars do not consider the body of law found in the various *fiqh* collections equivalent to Sharia. Quite the opposite: Most Muslim scholars, including those affiliated with the most

---

[48] See *wa-'l-sāriqu wa-'l-sāriqatu*...5:38.

conservative tendencies, emphasize that Sharia is that which is stated in the Quran and the Sunna, and that anything else is mere interpretation. However, even the most unambiguous passages of the Quran need human qualification in the form of definition, scope, and circumstance.

Confusion about the meaning and function of Sharia is often the outcome of uninformed commentators or reductionism: simplicity-driven theories. Abuse of Sharia in Muslim communities is also prevalent, in part due to willful ignorance of the first three centuries of Reasonists' contributions to law and jurisprudence, and in part due to the privileging of Traditionists' interpretations and applications of Islamic legal heritage. Traditionists claim that the Sunna and the Quran are the twin sources of Sharia. The first four caliphs and the Muslim jurists of the formative period are unlikely to have regarded the Sunna as a source of Sharia. Their practices and precedents suggest that they understood the Sunna as part of the body of *fiqh*, the same way they knew that their practice, too, was building the body of *fiqh*, not defining an immutable Sharia. The Sunna thus understood is interpretive, not legislative. Sharia, on the other hand, is legislative because it is rooted in the Quran.

Another general thought regarding Sharia is about its intimate connection to the political order during Islam's formative period. Many of legal rules and rulings were made part of the body that informs Sharia because they were enacted or enforced by key political figures, not because of sound legal reasoning, an established textual basis, or consensus among independent legal authorities. The first four caliphs played an especially unmatched role in defining and shaping Islamic law (*fiqh*), which Sharia reflects. For example, the rule of *`awl*, which is central to Sunni inheritance law, a fundamental institution with implications on property rights, became a legal principle not because it was based on explicit Quranic or Sunnaic text or broad consensus among jurists of that era, but rather because the second caliph, `Umar, imposed it. Therefore, one cannot understand the legal texts and legal theories that define

Sharia without understanding the origins, evolution, and functions of Islamic political order and political theory.

From the above discussion, I would propose a working definition of Sharia, which will allow the reader to identify the events and practices that make the Sharia what it has been throughout the history of Islamic thought and societies. A definition of Sharia that is useful must account for events and ideas from both the caliphate and post-caliphate era.[49]

Sharia is an oral[50] legal system rooted in the belief in a creator, and it derives its authority and power from this creator. The belief ensures the compliance of its adherents and subjects, is boosted by enticements and threats, and is empowered through reciprocal coupling of ethical and legal norms. Sharia is a multi-filter lens through which Muslims view and explain the world at any given moment, capturing judgements for any given occurrence. Muslims apply this multi-filter—including social, ethical, religious, psychological, political, and economic filters—to a specific case producing a legal judgment, augmenting the body of *fiqh*. Sharia, thus framed, is guideline-oriented where select cases represent the minimum entitlements when dealing with rights (e.g., inheritance rights) and

---

[49] It is a struggle to find meaningful demarcation points that allow for the distinction between circumstances and environments influencing the development of the idea and institution of Sharia. I am comfortable separating two distinct periods: the time during which Muslims lived under a pan-Islamic government that covered most Islamic lands, which is the time since the migration to Madīna until the dissolution of the Ottoman Sultanate, as being the caliphate era; and the post-caliphate era. Even this distinction is imprecise, because Muslims' attitudes toward many Islamic institutions began to change much earlier than the formal dissolution of the Ottoman Sultanate.

[50] It might be asked: If Sharia is derived from the Quran and the Sunna, and both the Quran and the Sunna are now written works, how can Sharia be oral? To answer that, the reader must recall that although the Quran is written down in collections called *muṣḥaf,* the Quran, for Muslims, is the recited (oral) tradition with all the elements that spoken words and gestures add to written words. The fact that Muslims refer to the written Quran as "*muṣḥaf*" instead of "the Quran" supports this conclusion. As for the Sunna, it should be recalled that *Hadith* was preserved and used orally for nearly three centuries before producing the various collections of *hadith*.

maximum punishments when dealing with crimes (e.g., killing). Sharia is akin to an instrument residing in the minds of jurists, whereas the content of *fiqh* is the outcome produced using Sharia, residing in various collections of law. Therefore, *fiqh* is a catalog of Sharia-aided snapshots related to theoretical cases, such as events occurring under normal circumstances, and abstract cases, such as fatwas. Sharia is many adaptable filters through which jurists pass information about any given case at any given time and in any society to determine the best judgment. Such a judgment may end up being purely moral, requiring no punishment; legal-related matters of worship, requiring no government policing or enforcement; or legal-related interpersonal transactions, requiring societal or governmental intervention in determining the form of redress and punishment (*ta`zīr*).

Sharia is often explained as a strict and harsh code of law. Human rights advocates often point to Sharia as a source of abuse in Islamic societies. They argue that Sharia allows torture, uses threats of torture, and sanctions punishments too harsh for modern times. Some Muslim thinkers and religious leaders challenge this assessment of Sharia as cultural imperialism; others call to reform Sharia, aligning it with norms of modernity and enlightenment. Both positions are flawed.

There is ample evidence that the West has, and continues to, pursue an imperial agenda when interacting with the rest of the world. The West is intent on preserving the dominance of its worldview. The question is not whether the West practices cultural imperialism; the question is whether Muslims believe in some form of human rights, independent of what the West does and wants. If Islam establishes a path towards greater respect for human dignity, then Muslim scholars and thinkers need to articulate that vision and those principles independent of any Western position or action.

Those who wish to reform Sharia to align it with the imperatives of the modern era are reactionaries. They wish to create a hybrid system that has elements of Sharia and elements of Western legal systems, and hope that this will solve the problem. Such a reform will not take hold, because any reformed system built on incompatible systems is inherently non-functioning. Western legal systems are built on norms that make them work. Sharia is also built on features that are necessary for it to work. Most importantly, Sharia is a system that combines both religious and secular aims, but the secular aims depend on the religious imperatives, practices, and doctrines. Sharia is a system, and if it is changed to adopt foreign elements and divest of its original elements, the result is a new system, not Sharia. Sharia's force is not in harsh sanctions and rigid punishments. Its force is in the threats and enticements not linked to any actual punishment or reward in this world. Sharia works because of its delayed punishment and reward, not its immediate swift justice. Any attempt to separate the two realms of Sharia would result in ending Sharia as a legal system. Therefore, Western ideas and instruments cannot vaccinate Sharia against human rights abuses. It either stands on its own as a system or is sidelined all together.

Sharia differs from modern legal systems. The latter are based on the power of the State, which is derived from society's norms and is dependent on strict enforcement of the law through coercion and financial incentives. Being a system, Sharia cannot be fully or partially implemented in a foreign environment. It requires all the elements that ensure its success, the same way a European legal system could not be successful in an environment designed for Sharia. A system, in this context, is a social environment containing all the forces and factors whose effects—without factoring in any outside forces—can generate an intelligible, quantifiable, and qualifiable social dynamic equilibrium.

Relevant to the rights equation I emphasize, governments exert power limited only by the law. In the case of classical Islamic political order, the caliphate, the Sunni pan-Islamic government, in theory[51] and in practice[52] has been built on a legitimacy extracted by dominance (*al-ghalaba*), not through a social contract. The dominance came from clan solidarity (*aṣabiyya*), grievance claims (*maẓlūmiyya*), or institutional military power (*askar; recall, mamluks*). Such a government cannot be trusted to promote the rights of the vulnerable or rights in general. Classical forms of government, notwithstanding their rootedness in a model of dominance, lacked the power to legislate, a void filled with Sharia, an elastic institution that is the domain of independent scholars employing *ijtihād* and guided by settled precedent (*ijmā`*). In other words, Islamic societies have more systems geared toward producing different outcomes than their counterparts in Western societies.

In this introduction, we have touched on the main themes with which Khallaf engages, albeit from a perspective that is rights-concerned and systems thinking-bound. Like Khallaf, I have considered social events to be turning points in history; they produce the context for change or for adoption of change in the areas of governance, jurisprudence, and judiciary.

Ahmed E. Souaiaia
University of Iowa
USA

---

[51] Ibn Khaldun, *al-Muqaddima* (Beirut: Dar al-kutub al-`ilmiyya, 195), 220.

[52] With the exception of the first thirty years, the majority of Islamic dynasties that governed over the pan-Islamic caliphate came into existence and preserved their rule on the basis of dominance—*ghalaba*.

The Legislative, Judicial, and Executive Branches in Islam

I

The Time of the Prophet

This period is characterized by the presence of the Messenger who was receiving revelations from God. It is relatively short, starting from the declaration of his Prophetship (*bi`tha*) in the year 610 CE until his demise in the year 632 CE. Technically, this period started when he migrated to Madīna in the year 622 CE and lasted until his demise, because during his stay in Mecca, his main objective was to propagate the divine message and to shield himself and his followers from oppression from the Quraysh. At this stage, the source of Islamic law was God and God alone.

Legislation During this Period

The first pillar of Islamic legislation is the Quran. The number of legal Quranic verses, however, does not exceed 200 verses, most of which were revealed after the migration (*hijra*), clarifying law in a particular event that already occurred or answering questions posed to the Messenger. These verses do not have the same style and mood for each instance in which they state the rules. The style varies because these verses were not only intended to decree or mandate laws, but also to express the inimitability (i`jāz) of the Quran, and to challenge experts and eloquent unbelievers to create something of its caliber. One example of the Quran's inimitability is its diversity in language style.

For instance, the Quran includes legal rulings in the form of affirmative or negative imperatives (*amr*), as it is the case in this verse:

Do marry what you elect from women; couplets, triplets, and quadruplets ... [4:3].

And this one:

Do not marry polytheists unless they believe ... [4:3].

In other verses, the law is in the form of an indicative statement (khabar), as was the case in this verse:

Divorced women shall wait three months ... [2:228].

And this one:

Mothers shall breastfeed their babies two full years for those who wish to finish suckling ... [2:233].

In a third example, the law is in the form of an answer to an inquiry (*istiftā'*), like this verse:

They ask you if war is permitted during the sacred month (al-shahr al-ḥarām); say: great wars during it ... [2:217].

And this verse:

They seek your ruling; say God will offer you a decree in [kalāla]; if a man dies and he does not leave behind a child and he has a sister, she shall inherit half of what he left behind ... [4:176].

And lastly, laws might be in the form of a clear prohibition or permission, as in this verse:

God has made trade legal and He prohibited usury ... [2:275].

And this verse:

It is prohibited for you (to marry) your mothers, your daughters, your sisters ... [4:23].

Some scholars have singled out these verses for standalone commentaries, including *al-Tafsīrāt al-aḥmadiyya*, and *Āyāt al-aḥkām* by al-Rāzī. Some scholars have looked at these verses from the point of view of their respective school of law (*al-madhhab al-fiqhī*), and have made it their objective to reconcile between these verses and what their scholars (*imāms*) have stated. This approach usually leads to errors.

A few notes are in order regarding the Quran's legislative verses:

1. Many of these verses embody stated laws as well as the wisdom behind the laws, and the public welfare that necessitated them. In other words, these verses state a ruling and provide its justification. These verses are not limited to a textual statement of laws, as is the case in this verse:

They ask you about menstruation, say it is harmful; therefore, stay away from women during menstruation until they become clean ... [2:222].

And this verse:

Surely Satan wants to cause amongst you enmity and contempt through wine and gambling, and wants to prevent you from the remembrance of God and from praying; so, are you going to stop ... [5:91].

And the verse concerning the waiting period of a divorced woman in her husband's house:

... She does not know, God might cause something to happen ... [65:1].

From this perspective, one may conclude that it is the responsibility of a legislator to explain the benefits that a ruling promotes or the harm it avoids to the governed public. Stating the law and the justification of the law ensures the law's adoption and application, and ensures that people will commit to the laws and honor them, even in the absence of enforcement institutions.

Moreover, providing the law and the justification of the law encourages independent thinking in order to produce laws that meet public welfare needs; since God's laws are justified by the needs of His servants, it follows that wherever exists benefits and well-being shall exist the law of God. In other words, God's laws exist as long as public welfare (*al-maṣlaḥa al-`āmma*) exists.

2. Many of the Quran's legislative verses offer a generalized version of the law without mentioning details, as is the case in the verse:

O! You who believe fulfill your contracts ... [5:1].

The above verse did not specify the type of contract, nor did it specify the type of obligations that must be recognized.

The verse "God has made trade legal and He has made usury prohibited ..." [2:275] also did not specify the usury that is illegal and the trade that is legal.

The verse below did not mention what is *ma`rūf*, what is *munkar*, what is *ṭayyib*, nor what is *khabīth.*

*Command them to enjoin what is good (*ma`rūf*), warn them against evil (*munkar*), make fine goods (*ṭayyibāt*) lawful for them, prohibit them from evils (*khabā'ith*), and disentangle them from their subconscious evil thoughts and its chains that enslaved them ...* [7:157]

The wisdom behind this generalization is to avoid discomfort that the text of the stated laws may cause. This vagueness may also allow for accommodation of all needs and details. Since it contains general legal principles for all people of all ages and all locations, it must accommodate their different needs. It also gives religious scholars more room to interpret these texts so that they are not discomforted by a necessity, nor prevented from providing for people's wellbeing. Avoiding details that some short-sighted individuals view as a handicap in legislation is in fact an example of Islamic ideals, and an exercise in perfection in the field of legal principles not limited to one nation or one epoch.

3. The number of verses that state laws—compared to the six thousand verses of the Quran—is very small, only about two hundred verses. The reason behind this is that the needs of early Muslims were limited. Their dealings with the law were also were limited because they were rural people and God legislated according to their needs and as necessitated for their welfare. Laws were stated in a manner that contained those needs and whatever could be a variant of those needs or related to them. The statements were also attached to general principles (*uṣūl*), in that they advocate the elimination of discomfort (*ḥaraj*) and detrimental acts, encourage

ease (*yusr*), and minimize the burden of excessive regulations and hierarchical authority. Furthermore, these laws were linked to justifying reasons, which in turn encouraged independent thinking and the use of analogy (*qiyās*).

Legislative verses in the Quran encompass general guidelines and the reasons behind particular legislation, so that laws do not exceed the exigencies of the people for whom they are made, and are not legislating theoretical issues or hypothetical situations. Along with laws, there should be a general ethical foundation to which people can refer in order to produce new laws for matters not addressed in the Book; hence legislation becoming an overall approach. Mentioning the rationale behind laws and the underlying reasons for these laws to be inscribed, and establishing general rules that go with these laws and general legislation, ensures that legislators cannot exclude a particular need in a particular age or particular place. These characteristics are summarized in the verse:

> *Today, I have perfected your religion for you, bestowed my blessing on you, and chosen Islam as a religion for you.* [5:3]

Legislative Prophetic Traditions

Legislative Traditions consist of the sayings and actions of the Messenger, through which he answered requests for a formal legal opinion or stated his point of view regarding a particular event. They are numerous, covering all aspects of life. They are, to some extent, similar in style and in approach to the legislative verses of the Quran. Some sayings consist of the statement of law as well as the justification of the stated law. In order to clarify this, we provide the following examples:

In matrimonial laws:

It is not permitted to marry at the same time a woman and her aunt (sister of her father or mother). If you do so, you cause the discontinuity of blood relation (qaṭ` al-raḥim) ...

On the prohibition of selling fruits before it ripens:

Do you see why God prohibited fruit (to be sold before it ripens)? So that no one of you will abuse the wealth of his brother.

On competition:

The believer is a brother of the believer: He shall not over-buy (by offering more money) that which his brother has bought, nor ask the hand of a woman who has been asked by his Muslim brother unless the latter cancels the engagement.

This style, as we mentioned regarding legislative verses, indicates permission to rely on independent thinking. It also rationalizes belief so that Muslims will obey these laws due to conviction rather than fear.

Other Traditions stated laws without any further elaboration. For example, the Tradition prohibiting dishonest trade (*bay` al-gharar*) does not define dishonesty:

Muslims recognize their terms (al-muslimūna `inda shurūṭihim) ...

And:

You shall not inflict harm on others nor on yourselves (lā ḍarara walā ḍirār).

Overall, these Traditions (a) clarify and detail laws stated in the Quran in a generalized form; and (b) state laws not prescribed in the Quran.

Most of the sayings and deeds of the Messenger were of the category that explained or clarified laws stated in the Quran. This assertion is further declared in the verse:

> *And we have revealed to you* dhikr *so that you may construe to people what was divulged for them.*

For instance, God commanded believers to perform prayers, give alms, perform pilgrimage, and fast during the month of Ramaḍān. The Messenger, on the other hand, simply clarified, through his words and deeds, the commands that were already stated in the Quran. For instance, regarding prayers, the Messenger said:

> *Pray the same way you see me pray.*

He also said:

> *Learn your rites (manāsik) from me.*

As a follow-up on the Quranic prohibition of usury, the Prophet said:

> A date for a date, salt for salt, an equal quantity for an equal quantity, a hand for a hand; then whoever increases or asks for an increase is committing usury. If you are dealing in things other than these things, then, trade any way you wish as long as it is a hand for a hand.

In expounding on God's prohibition of khabā'ith and legalization of *ṭayyibāt*, he cited rabbits and fish as examples of *ṭayyibāt*; and lions, some birds with talons, and domesticated donkeys as examples of *khabā'ith*.

Legislative aḥādīth concerning issues that were not dealt with in the Quran are extracted from Quranic general principles. When God prohibited simultaneous marriage to two sisters by one man, the Messenger followed up by prohibiting simultaneous marriage with a woman and her aunt (of either side of the parents) by one man using analogy:

> *If you do that then you cause the discontinuity of the blood relation.*

God also prohibited a man from marrying a woman who had breast-fed him (*ummāhāt min al-raḍā`a*) and women who were suckled with him (*akhawāt mina al-raḍā`a*). The Messenger, then, expanded the law to prohibit—similarly—marriage to an individual who is related through suckling (*taḥrīm mina al-raḍā`a*) and what is prohibited because of blood relation (*taḥrīm mina al-nasab*), using analogy between the mother and sister. Hence, all themes in the Sunna can be traced back to a text in the Quran or to part of its general fundamentals or to what was generally implied in its verses. Therefore, legislative verses are considered the first foundation for legislature, whereas legislative *aḥādīth* are considered the second foundation. One must not consult the Sunna for a formal legal opinion before consulting the Quran. This principle is further supported in the Tradition of Mu`ādh, when a judge was asked about his sources and he answered:

> *I refer to the Book of God; if I don't find (a supporting text), then I use the Sunna of His Messenger; if I don't find (a supporting text), then I use my own judgment (ijtihād).*

There is no dissent among Muslim scholars concerning the consideration of legislative *aḥādīth* as the second foundation of legislation.

Legislative *aḥādīth*, clarifying themes that in the Quran in general terms, were needed because an explanation must be appended to the text inscribed from God. God mandated giving alms (*zakā*);

the Messenger specified the tax brackets, nature of the taxable assets, the tax rate, and its time span and conditions. So not only should *zakā* be given, but also it must be given according to the guidelines determined by the Messenger.

As for legislative *aḥādīth* that state laws not mentioned in the Quran, these were accepted because they were extracted from the Quran using analogy (*qiyās*) or justified by the general fundamental principles it underscores. Prophetic Traditions were seen as such because the Messenger was illiterate and he could not have been able to initiate all these laws had he not been inspired by divine revelations. If he happened to err in his judgment, God voided his initiative. For example, the Messenger used his own logic and decided to accept ransom (*fidā'*) for prisoners of war after the battle of Badr; God overturned his decision and redirected him in the verse:

> *It is not for a Messenger to enthrall prisoners of war until he establishes himself (yathkhan) on earth. You want the worldly reward and God wants the hereafter for you...*

He also forgave people who did not report for war during the battle of Tabbūk, but God questioned that decision:

> *God forgave you when you permitted them ...*

In short, what was recorded from the Messenger in this context were either detailed laws expounding on generalized ones stated in the Quran, or laws that were in accordance with the comprehensive fundamental principles in the Quran. The importance of legislative *aḥādīth* is further reiterated in the following verses:

> *Enjoin that which the Messenger has permitted, and avoid that which you've been ordered to avoid.*

And:

> *And if you dispute (tanāza`tum) a matter, then do consult the Quran and the Sunna.*

Among the best books collecting and explaining indexed legislative *aḥādīth*, we mention *Nayl al-Awṭān* by al-Shawkānī. Ibn al-Qayyim mentioned in his book *A`lām al-muwaqi`īn* that the number of legislative *aḥādīth* does not exceed 4,500.

A Few Notes on Legislative *aḥādīth*

1. *Aḥādīth* were not recorded during the time of the Messenger, nor during the first century. In fact, the Messenger did not allow people to transcribe them and neither, after him, did his Companions. In other words, during this period, laws were contained in the Quran, which was revealed to the Messenger, who in turn recited it to his followers and dictated it to his scribes. The scribes then wrote on loose sheets, thus making the Quran the primary written as well as memorized source of legislation. Laws were also derived from the *aḥādīth*, memorized but not written down. These two sources then constituted the main foundation of the future legislature. In that, most differences between scholars were caused by the transmission of *aḥādīth*: Some *aḥādīth* were accepted by some and rejected by others. Other aḥādīth were rated sound (*saḥīḥ*) by a group of scholars and rated weak (*ḍa`īf*) by another. We could stipulate, then, that if these *aḥādīth* were recorded in a standard copy like the Quran and distributed among the peoples, we would have had a unique and single source of *aḥādīth*, hence the elimination of fabricated or forged Traditions. However, fearing that the *Ḥadīth* would be conflated or confused with the Quran prompted the Messenger to advise against transcribing *aḥādīth*. Such an action solved one problem but created another.

2. People who had memorized these *aḥādīth* were not required to narrate them verbatim. Rather, the Companions reported the meaning of the *aḥādīth*, in some cases using their own words. Thus, the syntax of a single *Ḥadīth* may differ from one narrator to another. *Ḥadīth ḥajjat al-wadā`*, for example, was narrated multiple times, each time using different vocabulary. This problem expanded to influence legislation afterwards, because the meaning of the *Ḥadīth* changed as its vocabulary changed.

3. Legislative *aḥādīth* were not induced by the Messenger's independent thinking alone; rather, they were sometimes induced in consultation with some of his Companions. It was reported that once he said, describing Mecca:

> "Its desert is never empty, and its trees are never dry." al-Abbās said: "Except *al-athkhar*" (a type of plant), then the Messenger continued: "Except *al-athkhar*."

There is no doubt that the consideration of public welfare—introducing consultative (*shūra*) methods and by institutionalizing independent thinking—enhanced people's conditions, traditions, and dealings during the process of legislation. For that reason, knowledge of Arab customs and traditions was necessary at this early stage in order to help them understand these laws. Knowledge of the causes of revelation of legislative verses and the events that triggered a legislative *Ḥadīth* guided future scholars to the truth as they extracted new laws and justified the already-stated ones.

Ibn al-Qayyim, in his book *A`lām al-muwaqi`īn*, wrote:

The Sunna vis-à-vis the Quran had to fulfill three things:

1. The Sunna must conform to the Quran in all aspects, so that they have the same opinion regarding the same issue, since the justifications are the same.

2. The Sunna must clarify what was stated in the Quran and explain it.

3. The Sunna can only prohibit matters not prohibited in the Quran and legalize matters not legalized in the Quran. The Sunna, then, cannot be anything other than what was mentioned above, and cannot contradict the Quran. As he (the Messenger) said, God gave him the authority to legislate what was not legislated as well as He authorized him to clarify what God wanted him to clarify. For that, everything the Messenger stated is from God, and any addition is by no means separate from that which was stated in the Quran.

From what we have previously said, it is clear that during this period only the Messenger had the authority to legislate. He exerted this authority without the participation of any of his Companions, and his source was divine revelations and inspirations. He legislated by declaring topics and texts that his Lord revealed to him in accordance with the verse:

> *O! Messenger; deliver what has been revealed to you from your Lord. If you don't, then you did not fulfill your mission.*

His act of legislation was also manifested in his explanation of the revealed verses:

> *And we have revealed to you* dhikr, *so that you may explain to people what has been sent down for them.*

Finally, he legislated as an independent thinker (*mujtahid*). He extracted laws that were not revealed in the Quran by relying on divine revelations and by considering the welfare of the people. Legislation was not a one-time statement; rather, it was a gradual process occurring across different occasions and events throughout the 22 years from his declaration as Messenger until his demise.

The individuals who were recognized as *muftīs* during this period—like the four righteously guided caliphs, including Abdullah Ibn Mas`ūd, and Abdul Raḥmān Ibn `Awf— had a limited number of rulings that hardly exceeded the simple attempt and effort to comprehend the texts they had memorized. They also explained these texts to those who did not comprehend them. But they never exceeded their limit to extract or issue formal legal opinions that were not mentioned in the Quran or in the Sunna. This was the case because the Messenger—to whom they returned for all inquiries—was still with them.

In the case where one of them took an independent action or stated his own decree, that ruling did not have any power unless the Messenger confirmed it, and once he did, it became legislation from the Messenger, for he was the one who made it official. It is for this reason that many Muslim scholars view Traditions from the Companions with the same weight.

Characteristics of This Period

This legislative period stands unique for the following reasons:

1. During this time, it was never the case where a law was disputed, nor were there ever two or more opinions concerning a single issue. Because only one individual had had the power to legislate, his opinion was decisive, and he was the final arbiter and interpreter of the Quran laws when one needed to understand a text or seek a formal legal opinion. This man was the Messenger [PBUH] and his source of law was the divine revelations.

2. Only legislative verses were written down during this period. These verses were not published and were not accessible to everyone. Only selected scribes and individuals wrote down copies of

the Quran. The rest of the people were taught to memorize it. Legislative *aḥādīth,* however, were never written down at this time; they spread only by transmission of oral reports.

3. Legislation, at this time, was in the form of responses to events that took place, and only responded to the needs and provided for the welfare of the people. The legislative texts were generally spiritual, aimed at preaching to people of the good and prosperity they contained. Also, these texts tended to stress belief or faith as the foundation of law, so that conformity stemmed from conviction rather than fear of punishment or coercion.

Jurisprudence during This Period

The judicial branch—as was the case with the executive branch—was in the hands of the Messenger [PBUH], a power delegated to him by God:

> *Govern them according to what God has revealed, and do not follow their wishes instead of what has come onto you from the Truth.*

And:

> *Nay! By your Lord, they shall not be considered believers, unless they choose you as the judge to settle their disputes without being annoyed or discomforted by your decision, and unless they submit fully.*

During this time period, it was the Messenger [PBUH] who was in charge of the legislative branch; he also appointed others to serve as judges. Evidence of his authority can be concluded from the following sound Traditions:

Imām Aḥmad reported in his *Musnad* on the authority of Umm Salmah, Hind, and the wife of the Messenger [PBUH] who said:

> Two men came to the Messenger [PBUH] disputing the distribution of an inheritance and neither of them had proof one way or the other. The Messenger [PBUH] said: "You have brought your dispute to the Messenger. I'm a human being. Maybe one of you is more eloquent and presents his argument better than the other. Be aware that I will make my decision given what I hear. So if I give one of you from the right of his brother, he should not take it, because it is nothing but a piece from the fire which he will carry around his neck until the Day of Judgment." The two men cried and both decided to give up whatever rights they may have had. The Messenger [PBUH] then said: "Now, go and divide (the inheritance) and take each other as true brothers, and take your shares and ask each other for forgiveness."

Mohammed Ibn al-Ḥasan said: "Abu Ḥanīfa had told us on the authority of Ḥammād, on the authority of Ibrāhīm al-Nakh`ī, that a man married a woman without giving her a dowry, then he died before consummation (before *dukhūl*). Abdullah Ibn Mas`ūd decreed that she should have a dowry like other women, no more, no less." After making his decision he said: "If this is the right decision, it is from God; if it is wrong, then it is from Satan. God and his Messenger are not responsible. A man who was in his circle said, "We have heard that this man was Ma`qal Ibn Sinān al-Ashjā`ī." A Companion of the Messenger said: "By the One we swear by, you have made the same decree the Messenger stated in the case of Berū' Bint Wāshiq al-Ashja`iyah." He said that Abdullah was so happy because his decree conformed to that of the Messenger [PBUH].

Mālik reported in his *Muwatta*: A grandmother came to Abu Bakr asking him about her share in inheritance. He said: "Nothing for you according to the Quran, and we don't know of anything in the Sunna either. Go home and wait for me until I ask people." He said: "He asked people and al-Mughīra Ibn Shu`ba said: 'The Messenger has given her the sixth.' Abu Bakr asked: 'Can anyone else confirm this?' al-Mughīra replied: 'Mohammed Ibn Muslimah.' who confirmed al-Mughīra's story. Then Abu Bakr gave her the sixth."

The other grandmother came to Umar Ibn al-Khaṭṭāb requesting her inheritance. Umar said: "According to the Quran, you do not have any share. And the previous decree was for someone else. I will not add a thing to the official shares. It is only the sixth. If both of you demanded it at the same time you would have shared it. Since she came first, then it will be hers."

As for the Prophet's appointment of other judges during his lifetime, a number of aḥādīth were stated in this regard:

Imām Aḥmad and Abu Dawūd have narrated on the authority of Mu`ādh Ibn Jabal, who said that when he was appointed judge of Yemen the Messenger asked him: "How would you reach a decision if a case is to be presented to you?" He replied: "I consult the book of God." The Messenger said: "What if you don't find (anything)?" He said: "Then I consult the Sunna of his Messenger." The Messenger continued: "What if you don't find (a ruling) in the Sunna of His Messenger nor in His book?" He replied: "Then I use my own judgment." He said: "When he heard this, the Messenger put his hand on his chest and said: "Praise be to God who guided the messenger of the Messenger of God to what pleases the Messenger of God."

Abu Dawūd narrated on the authority of Ali Ibn Abi Ṭālib who said:

The Messenger of God sent me to Yemen as a judge though I was young and I had no experience in judgeship and said: "Indeed God will guide your heart and make your speech firm. If two individuals bring before you a dispute, do not make a final decision until you hear from both sides; that is better for you since the truth will be clearer." He said, "I'm still a judge and I never doubted a decision I have made so far."

When God freed Mecca for the Muslims, the Messenger appointed `Utāb Ibn Asīd al-Qurashī al-Umawī, who remained there as a governor and judge until he died during the last days of Abu Bakr's caliphate.

Traditions confirm that the Messenger himself undertook the judiciary branch and he appointed some of his Companions to serve in that branch. There is no evidence, though, that he ever appointed an individual solely as a judge. In fact, it is evident that he sent individuals as his messengers and representatives. They taught people, gave formal opinions, acted as judges, and collected *zakā*. In other words, these representatives had a holistic role, rather than being restricted to judgeship. In other words, during the time of the Messenger, judgeship was not separated from governorship because its duties were so few. But after this time period, when the number of Muslims increased and the duties of governors became more and more complex, a division emerged between judgeships and governorships. Furthermore, even the judgeship itself was divided between politically appointed judges and private judges.

It was reported that the Messenger [PBUH] appointed someone as a judge and only a judge on a particular dispute (as a special counsel). Abu `Amr Ibn Abdul Barr mentioned in *al-Isti`āb*, on the authority of Jariyah Ibn |afar, [RAA] that a house was shared between two brothers, who built a wall and then both died, leaving two heirs. Each of the two heirs claimed that the wall was his and only his. So they brought the matter before the Messenger [PBUH], who sent Ḥudhayfa al-Yamamī to be the judge in this matter. After ruling that the wall belonged to the person who had grown lettuce next to the wall, Ḥudhayfa returned and reported the decision to the Messenger [PBUH]. The Messenger said: "You've done well, you ruled correctly..."

From the above Traditions, we can conclude that the Messenger did not have a systematic approach in appointing judges; he appointed individuals as judges and governors at the same time. Especially when he left Madīna for war, he chose someone to replace him as he did during Ghazwat al-Abwāb, when he appointed Sa`d Ibn Ubādah, and during Ghazwat Bawat he appointed al-Sayib Ibn Madh'un. When a new city fell under Islamic rule, he also left someone there as his representative, like `Utāb Ibn Asīd, the governor of Mecca, Abu Mūsā al-Ash`arī, and Mu`ādh Ibn Jabal, the governor of Yemen. These and others were employed so that these regions would not fall into anarchy and chaos. He [PBUH] also appointed special counsels for specific cases and particular disputes, as in the case of the disputed wall.

For this reason, it is not possible to determine the number of individuals who were judges during the time of the Messenger [PBUH], because judgeship at this time was either all-encompassing and incorporated into the governorship, or limited to specific cases. For those who served on specific cases, their appointment automatically terminated once the case was solved. Hence, if history reports that Umar or Ali [RAA] served as judges during the time of the Messenger [PBUH], their roles should not be understood in a context different from that of the appointment of Hudhayfah, who served as a special counsel on specific cases, or that of `Utāb Ibn Asīd in Mecca or Mu`ādh Ibn Jabal and Abu Mūsā al- Ash`arī in Yemen, who consolidated judgeship and governorship as decided by the Messenger [PBUH].

All appointments made by the Prophet, then, included general governorship or the limited authority of special counsels. For example, in the Tradition of Hudhayfah, the Messenger appointed him to settle a dispute between two specific individuals in a specific case. Regarding the appointment, `Utāb, al-Zamakhsharī wrote in *al-Kishāf* that the Messenger appointed `Utāb Ibn Asīd and told him: "Go, I appointed you governor over the people of the house of God." So this was an all-encompassing governorship.

A closer reading of the judicial rulings shows that judgeship of this period was more of a statement of formal opinion (*iftā'*). A judge was more expected to know the divine law than pronounce it. Rather, most of the cases brought before judges were quests for formal opinions regarding specific issues. This is evident from the tradition reported by Bukhārī on the authority of `Ā'isha [RAA], who narrated that Hind Bint `Utba, the wife of Abu Sufyān, told the Messenger:

"Indeed Abu Sufyān is a stingy man; he does not give me and my son what we need, except that which we take without his knowledge." He replied: "Take what you need for yourself and for your son with fairness."

The scholars of Islamic law have considered this Tradition to be a judicial statement; in reality, it is a formal opinion.

Since seeking a judicial settlement was a form of seeking a formal religious opinion (*istiftā'*) during this time, the process did not follow specific guidelines. In fact, we know nothing about this process except that which was reported by Imām Aḥmad and Ibn Dawūd:

If two individuals bring between your hands a dispute, do not make a final decision until you hear from both sides. That is better for you since the truth will be clearer.

And the Tradition:

You are seeking my judgment and I'm but a human...

Also we do not know about the rules of evidence except through the few Traditions reported by Bukhārī and Muslim in the authority of Ibn Abbās, where the Messenger said:

If people were given everything they claim, they will seek the blood and wealth of each other. For that the accuser must provide proof or evidence.

Al-Bayhaqī also narrated:

The plaintiff must provide evidence. If the defendant denies, then he must take an oath.

The most distinctive characteristic of the judicial system during this period was the independence of the judge. It is clear from the Tradition previously reported that the Messenger did not put any restraints on the judges and governors he appointed. In fact, he simply told Hudhayfah: "Go and settle this dispute between them. He said to `Utāb Ibn Asīd: "Go—I have appointed you to the people of the house of God." He also approved the criterion of Mu`ādh, and gave general advice to Ali [RAA]. All these appointees were expected to use the Quran, the Sunna, and—in the event they did not find clear supporting text in these two sources—then they used their own independent thinking. In other instances, the Messenger approved or disapproved their decisions as mentioned in the *Ḥadīth* of Hudhayfah, when he reported back to the Messenger, who [PBUH] told him that he had made the correct decision. Regarding the requirement of evidence, they demanded proof from the plaintiff and an oath from the defendant if he denied the charges. The judge may have required evidence from both sides, as we have seen in the case of the wall. The general rule followed by all of these judges was that stated in the Quran:

> *Indeed God commands you to return to its rightful owners that which was entrusted to you; and if you were to settle a dispute among people you shall be just and fair.*

Abu Dawūd also narrated on the authority of Buraydah, who reported that the Messenger [PBUH] said:

> Judges are of three kinds: two in hell and only one in paradise; a man who knows the truth and rules accordingly, he will enter paradise. A man who knows the truth but does not rule accordingly, he will enter

> hell. And a man who does not know the truth and rules among people despite his ignorance, he will enter hell.

Some historical documents from this time period show that the judge stated the law and executed it himself or appointed a deputy who would carry out the execution. The following Tradition was reported in *Ṣaḥīḥ Muslim* and *Ṣaḥīḥ Bukhārī*:

> Two men came to seek legal opinion from the Messenger [PBUH]. One of them told the Messenger: "Settle this matter between us according to the book of God." The second person—who was more learned in Islamic law—added: "Yes, Messenger of God, settle this matter between us according to the Book of God and allow me to say something." The Messenger said: "Say what you wish to say." The second man continued: "My son was employed by the family of this man, then he fornicated with his wife. So I agreed to give him hundred sheep and a servant. I also asked some erudite people and they told me that my son must be subjected to flogging (one hundred times) and exiled for one year. As for the wife of this man, she must be stoned." The Messenger said: "I swear by the one who has my life in His hands, I will settle this matter between you according to the book of God. The hundred sheep and the servant are not acceptable. As for your son, he must be flogged one hundred times and exiled for one year. Go, Anīs, to his wife and ask her; if she confesses, then stone her." He asked her and she confessed, then he stoned her.

The collectors of Traditions also reported that while Ṣafwān Ibn Umayya was asleep in the mosque of the Messenger [PBUH] on a piece of his clothes, a thief came and stole it. When he caught him he took him to the Messenger [PBUH], who ordered his hand cut.

Safwān then said: "O Messenger! Do you cut his hand because he stole my dress? I am giving it to him." The Messenger said: "Why did not you forgive him before you brought him to me?"

Executive Decisions during This Time Period

We define executive decisions as all actions required by the politics of Muslims and how they go about their affairs besides legislation and judiciary. During his time as Prophet, the Messenger held executive power as well as judicial and legislative powers. Given the exceptional role he was given as God's Messenger, it was necessary that he supervise the three branches; as a Messenger, he was passing on to the people what was revealed to him from his Lord and inviting them to believe in Him. As a politician, he put in effort to organize his community and oversee their affairs in the light of what God legislated. The net of these activities constituted legislative, judicial, and executive roles. The fact that these three powers were in the hands of one person did not cause any danger that may have necessitated their separation, because he [PBUH] was infallible (*ma`ṣūm*) and guarded from undertaking an action based on his personal interests or his personal desires. In summary, we can say that he did not share legislative power with anybody; he played the role of the ultimate judge although he appointed others to that position, as we have explained. Finally, he served as the chief executive and he appointed others to secondary executive positions.

In his book, *Nihāyat al-Ījāz fī sīrati sākinī al-Ḥijāz,* in the section "Takhrīj al-Dalā'il al-Sam`iyyah," the late Rifa`ah Bic Rāfi' introduced a summary of the posts and positions that existed during the time of the Messenger and the people who were appointed to hold military, financial, or religious positions. He mentioned the ministry (*wizāra*), the chief of staff (*hijāba*), secretariat (*kitāba*), water distribution (*siqāya*), natural resources (*sadāna*), Pilgrimage leadership (*imārat al-Ḥajj*), Prayers leadership (*imāmat al-Ṣalāh*), teaching the Quran (*ta`līm al-qur'ān*), jurisprudence (*fiqh*), judicial sector (*qaḍā'*), documentation (*tawthīq*), inheritance distributor (*fāridh al-mawārīth*), pensions (*nafaqāt*), shares (*al-aqsām*), accountant (*al-muḥtasib*), announcer (*munādī*), city guard (*ḥāris al-madīna*), prison guard (*al-sajjān*), and law executors (*muqīmī al-ḥudūd*), among others. The list of these positions is more than two hundred pages long.

As examples, we will enlist the organization of some executive affairs during the time of the Messenger: military affairs, financial affairs, and execution of the laws. Those who wish for more details and further research may consult the book we mentioned above.

During the time of the Messenger [PBUH], military affairs were limited to fighting pagans who stood as hurdles in the way of the Islamic Invitation. An *amīr* headed each Islamic group going to war. If the Messenger [PBUH] was leaving with the troops, then he was the *amīr*. If he was staying, he chose someone else to be the *amīr* of the army. The Messenger had led the armies twenty six times (*ghazwa*) during his lifetime. He appointed an *amīr* for more than 56 *sariyya*. The appointed *amīr* was not restricted to commanding the troops militarily; rather, he also led the prayers, executed laws, and oversaw all of the troops' affairs. The *amīr*, including the Messenger, consulted experts and ranking officers and did not make decisions without consultation.

It was reported that during one of the wars, the Messenger [PBUH] ordered the troops to camp in a particular place. One of his companions asked him if this was an order from God or a military maneuver. When the Messenger [PBUH] replied that it was a military opinion not inspired by God, the Companion objected to it and eventually the Messenger changed his instructions and followed his Companion's advice.

In *Ṣaḥīḥ Muslim*, Buraydah Ibn al-Khaṭīb's authority is recorded as reporting that the Messenger [PBUH] advised the *amīr*, saying:

> Fight in the name of God for the cause of God. You ought to fight whomever disbelieves in God. You shall not surprise or mutilate your enemy and you shall not kill youngsters.

So in short, the Messenger was the commander-in-chief. If he were among the fighting troops, he was the executive commander-in-chief. If not, then he designated someone to oversee all of the military affairs of the troops. The appointed *amīr* then led, but he generally consulted the ranking officers before making any major decisions.

As for financial affairs, during this time they were limited to administrating the three revenue-generating areas:

1. War-generated revenues (that which was captured during war, aka *ghanā'im*),
2. Fines and fees (*fī'*), and
3. Alms and taxes (*zakā*).

The administrators managed the distribution of generated money as determined in the Quran.

Ghanā'im were distributed as stated in chapter (*sūra*) al-Anfāl:

Do know that what you've collected (from war) for God the fifth ...

al-Fī' was that which was taken from non-Muslims in the absence of war (*jizya*). It was distributed as stated in chapter al-Ḥashr:

> And what God has bestowed on his Messenger from them, you did not tire your horses over it ...

Zakā was the taxes on money, cattle, land, and fruit. It was spent or distributed according to the instructions found in chapter al-Tawba:

> *Indeed, the alms are for the poor, the needy, those in charge of its collection ...*

The Messenger [PBUH] also used to designate one person—known as *ṣāḥib al-maghānim*

1 Figure

—to collect and account for ghanā'im during wars so that it was distributed fairly. It was narrated by Wahb Ibn Munabbih on the authority of a man from Quraysh who said:

When the Messenger [PBUH] surrounded Khaybar, some people were so hungry. When part of the city gave up to the Muslim army, one of the Muslims took a pocket of fat but was seen by the person in charge of *ghanā'im*, Ka`b Ibn `Amr Ibn Zayd al-Anṣārī, who took it from him, but the Messenger [PBUH] said: "Let him go with his pocket." The man left and shared it with his companions.

The day of the Battle of Yarmūk, the person in charge of *ghanā'im* was Abu Sufyān Ibn Ḥarb. As for the battle of Ḥunayn, Mas`ūd Ibn `Amr al-Qāri' was *ṣāḥib al-ghanā'im*.

The revenues of war, or *fī'*, were distributed immediately. Abu `Ubayd al-Qāsim Ibn Salām narrated on the authority of al-Ḥasan Ibn Mohammed that the Messenger [PBUH] never kept money with him or in his house. In other words, if money was received in the morning, he dispersed it before noon, and if it came in the afternoon, he did not go to bed before distributing it. Abu Dawūd also narrated on the authority of Hawf Ibn Mālik that the Messenger [PBUH] used to distribute *fī'* as soon as it reached him. For that reason, there was no treasury during his time, nor was there an agency to manage the finances of the state; money was always distributed as soon as the Prophet received it.

It is reported that a person oversaw *ghanā'im* and *fī'* until it was distributed. Similarly, the *jizyah* was administered by an agent who was responsible for its collection and distribution. It was narrated that once the Messenger [PBUH] reached a truce with the people of Najrān and Baḥrayn, he immediately appointed the "honest of the Ummah"—`Ubaydullah Ibn al-Jarrā—to collect the fees from them. When he [PBUH] appointed Mu`ādh Ibn Jabal as governor on Yemen, he also instructed him to collect one *dinar* or its equivalent from each adult. Other agents were also in charge of charity and alms collection. Ibn Isḥāq reported in *al-Siyar* that the Messenger [PBUH] used to send his envoys and governors—who could not be counted—to all the lands ruled by Islam. Amongst them: Umar, Khālid Ibn Sa`īd, Mu`ādh Ibn Jabal, and Ubay Ibn Ka`b.

Alms collected by agents were given to another agent called the *mustawfī*, who brought it to the Messenger. For instance, the Messenger sent Ali [RAA] to Najrān to receive whatever was collected from them as alms by `Amr Ibn Ḥazm and as *jizyah* by Ubaydah Ibn al-Jarrāḥ.

Alms were then distributed as ordered in the Quran. It was narrated that two men asked the Messenger [PBUH] if they could receive some money from the alms and he replied:

> God did not delegate the appropriation of alms (*ṣadaqāt*) to Prophets nor to anyone else. God mandated their distribution to people who belong to one of the eight social groups; if you are eligible to receive any portion, I will give it to you.

Concerning the laws, what can be concluded from the overall Traditions is that laws of legalization, prohibition, duties, and civil rights did not need in its entirety an executor besides concerned individuals, since they were mostly a matter of questions by some people who acted according to the formal opinion issued by the Prophet upon their request. The judge or whomever the judge appointed to execute the law enforced laws requiring an executor—like punishments. This area of law did not have specifically appointed agents; rather, all Muslims were expected to execute laws once they were selected for such a duty. As we have seen in the Tradition of al-Asīf where the Messenger [PBUH] said: "Go Anīs to the woman and ask her; if she confesses, then stone her." So Anīs was none but one of the members of general public who witnessed this process and was chosen to execute the law.

One of the most obvious acts of executive undertaking during this epoch was the designation of governors over states that accepted Islam. These governors were given general powers, enabling them to administer the affairs of citizens of that particular geographical area. When the Messenger left Madīna for a military mission, he appointed a successor. Similarly, once a city accepted Islam, he left a representative to govern on his behalf. For example, he designated `Utāb Ibn Asīd governor of Mecca, Uthmān Ibn Abi al-`Āṣ governor of Tā'if, Ali, Mu`ādh Ibn Jabal, and Abu Mūsā al-Ash`arī governors of Yemen, and `Āmr Ibn Ḥazm governor of Najrān. These governors had authority not only to govern but also to serve as judges, to execute laws, to collect alms and fees, and to defend the land and people in case of an invasion. For this reason, historians are in disagreement regarding the responsibilities of such appointed individuals: whether they were judges, agents who collect alms and fees, or leaders of the obligatory prayers.

The Messenger chose governors amongst those well-known for being strong and honest. Imām Muslim narrated on the authority of Abu Dharr [RAA], who said:

I asked the Messenger: "Don't you want me for governorship?" The Messenger put his hand on my knee and said: "O! Abu Dharr, you are weak, and it is governorship! When the Day of Judgment comes, you will regret the day you took it. Governorship will humiliate anyone except those who were righteous in using it and honest in fulfilling their duties while in it."

The Messenger also determined the wages of his governors and held them accountable for even the gifts they received. It was narrated in *Ṣaḥīḥ Muslim* and *Ṣaḥīḥ al-Bukhārī* on the authority of Abu Hamīd al-Sa`dī, who said:

> The Messenger appointed a man from al-Azd called Ibn al-Latība to collect alms. Upon reporting to Madīna, he gave some to the Messenger and kept

> some, claiming it as gift given to him. The Messenger [PBUH] then said: “What happened! Some man, whom we put in charge of some of responsibilities delegated to us by God, comes to us and says this is for you and this was given to me as gift! Why doesn't he stay in his father's house or mother's house and see if anyone would give him gifts then!”

In conclusion, one could say that there is no doubt that the Messenger did not die until he proclaimed the message, legislated according to what was revealed to him and according to his independent thinking, served as a judge among the people, and governed Muslims along with some of his helpers. He brought a strict religion and founded a strong nation. His work in legislative, judiciary, and executive areas was that of a Messenger from God who governed humanity according to God's laws.

II

The Period of the Companions

This time period extends from the demise of the Messenger [PBUH] in the year 11 *Hijrī* (H.) to the turn of the century: nearly 90 years. What is of importance here is the fact that none of the sources of law besides the Quran were ever written down. Certainly, Neither the Sunna nor the independent thinking of the *mujtahids* were recorded. Legislation and judicial matters—from anywhere in the Islamic land—were brought to the attention of the Companions of the Messenger. These Companions, who were prepared to state formal opinions, lived during most of the hundred years after *Hijrah*, including Anas Ibn Mālik, who died in the year 93 H. Hence this period was dubbed the Period of Companions (*ʿahd al-ṣaḥāba*).

Legislation During This Time Period

We have already established that during the time of the Messenger [PBUH], no one but him enjoyed legislative power. There were two sources for legislation: God's revelations and the Messenger's independent thinking. After his demise, the process of revelation ceased and his independent thinking ended. People in charge of the affairs of Muslims consulted legislative verses in the Quran as well as legislative *aḥādīth* whenever they needed a ruling concerning a particular issue. However, since these texts were—to some extent—answers to specific events that occurred in the past or answers to the needs of the first generation of the Muslim community, the rulings contained therein were meant for what had already happened, not what was happening now or what would happen in the future.

As the message of Islam spread, more people of different customs and traditions assimilated into the larger Muslim community. This expansion brought within its fold different customs, political order, traditions, social and ethnic diversity, and new political and economic factors that were not present during the time of the Messenger. In this new situation, Muslim scholarship was left with one of two options:

1. Resort to a third source of legislation from which they could extract Islamic laws and decrees regarding issues not solved by legislative texts. Or,

2. Choose a group of people to interpret the previously mentioned (two) sources and derive new rulings, so that Islam could continue to provide relevant answers to novel questions in a fast-growing community, ensuring the continuity of the Islamic legislative movement as the *Umma* progressed and developed.

Sources of Legislation during this Period

Muslim scholars resorted to a third source of legislation known as *ijtihād* (independent thinking). It consisted of drawing analogies between issues and cases in the two primary sources of law and issues for which legal formal opinion was sought. The Messenger himself guided scholars to this avenue through his actions and sayings, since he himself exerted independent thinking on a number of occasions and he used analogy to extrapolate laws to similar cases. This was evident from his prohibition of simultaneous marriage with a woman and her aunt, hinting to the analogy by saying: "If you do that you cause discontinuity in the blood relation..." He also prohibited daughters (through suckling), as analogous to God's prohibition of a mother (who breastfed the man seeking her hand in marriage), since both cases shared the same factor. Furthermore, the Messenger [PBUH] explained the reasons behind laws as if he were telling people that these laws were to protect and provide for the welfare of society at large, rather than add more burdens on individuals. He also approved of the independent thinking of a number of his Companions during his lifetime. Furthermore, he stated that the *mujtahid* would be rewarded regardless of the results of his efforts; rewarded twice if he reached the right decision or rewarded once if he erred. His interview of Mu`ādh Ibn Jabal before sending him to Yemen also legitimized and set guidelines for the *mujtahids*.

The above actions of the Messenger [PBUH] and other *aḥādīth* and verses guided his successors to adopt a third source of legislation: *ijtihād*. God also says in the Quran:

If you dispute any matter, do consult God and His Messenger...

And:

If they consult the Messenger and those in charge amongst them, that which they dispute will be clear to them ...

So, successors consulted the Quran, the legislative *aḥādīth*, then—in cases where they did not find a ruling concerning the issue at hand—they used analogy to extract a new ruling.

In summary, the sources of legislation at this time were three: (1) the Quran, (2) the Sunna, and (3) independent thinking (*ijtihād*) of scholars among the Companions of the Messenger [PBUH]. Some people add to this list consensus (*ijmā`*), which is not appropriate since consensus is not a source of law, as scholars reach consensus after they refer to a text in the Quran or the Sunna. Thus, the source would be the text used and not their consensus. In other words, consensus is a proof of the validity of a particular law, but not a source of law per se.

Legislators of This Period

The individuals who held legislative roles were a handful of the Messenger's Companions who had lived with him for a protracted period of time, and who were well-known for their scholarship and capacity to memorize the Quran and *aḥādīth*. They were known as the jurist Companions (*fuqahā' al-Ṣaḥāba*). They lived in different parts of the Muslim world. A large number of Muslims consulted them whenever they needed a formal opinion, hence this class of jurists were looked to as people of the legislative branch of that time period. The most famous of them all were:

- In Madīna: The four righteously guided caliphs, Zayd Ibn Thābit, and Abdullah Ibn Mas`ūd.
- In Basra: Anas Ibn Mālik and Abu Mūsā al-Ash`arī.
- In Shām: Mu`ādh Ibn Jabal and Ubādah Ibn al-Ṣāmiṭ.
- In Egypt: Abdullah Ibn `Amr Ibn al-`Āṣ.

Besides these prominent scholars, other Companions and their students also were known to issue formal opinions as reported by Ibn al-Qayyim, who reported that the number of people who offered formal legal opinions during this time exceeded 135 men and women. Nonetheless, those mentioned remained the most prominent legislators as well as the ultimate judges. Governors and designated judges sought their final ruling in complex cases.

It is worth mentioning at this juncture that none of these individuals earned the title of "legislator" as a result of their succession of the Messenger (as caliphs) or because they were elected as such. Rather, it was because of the amount of the Quran they had memorized, their deep knowledge of the meaning and spirit of legal principles found in the Quran and the Sunna, and their long companionship to the Messenger [PBUH]. The majority of Muslims recognized these qualities in them to the extent that these individuals became the only legislators.

Approaches and Jurisdictions

The dominions of the early jurists were limited because they were not to override a law already stated in the Quran or in the Sunna. They could only interpret the texts of the Quran and the *Ḥadīth* to clarify the focus and the implications of stated laws. In the case of a lack of textual evidence concerning particular issues, their prerogative was limited to establishing an analogy to link issues that lacked legal clearance with those that addressed in the Quran or the Sunna. Their role, then, consisted of searching for common reasons behind a prohibition or legalization. We must add that none of these *mujtahids* ever held the right to state a primary law that could not be supported by the Quran and the Sunna. In this early stage, the consensus of the Companions (as a group) was the only form of legislative process. Later, individuals were able to legislate.

Legislation by Committee

During the caliphate of Abu Bakr and the first half of `Umar's caliphate, legislators convened as a group before issuing any law. This was possible since the land ruled by Islam was limited to the Arabian Peninsula and the scholars lived within relatively close proximity to one another. Thus, they were able to gather every time an issue was brought forth. Eventually, legislation—whether an interpretation of text or a pronouncement of new laws extracted using analogy—was issued as the opinion of their committee, not of an individual.

This fact can be supported by the Tradition narrated by al-Bahwī on the authority of Maymūn Ibn Mahrān, who said:

If a dispute is brought to the attention of Abu Bakr, he looks in the book of God; if he finds a solution in it, he makes his decision accordingly; if nothing related to the dispute is found in the book, he considers a Prophetic Tradition that he knew and he uses it to make his decision. If not, he presents the case to the people and asks if anyone knows a statement from the Messenger [PBUH] in this regard. Generally, a number of people will gather to recite what they learned from the Messenger. After which, Abu Bakr concludes by saying: "Praise be to God who made among us someone who memorizes the sayings of our Messenger." But in the case where there is no evidence from the Sunna, he gathers the most learned individuals and consults them. If they reach a consensus, he uses their decision. `Umar, after him, has followed the same procedure; if he fails to find something in the Quran and the Sunna, he looks to see if Abu Bakr made a decision in a similar case; if not, he gathers the learned scholars and uses their consensus as his final decision.

It is obvious from this Tradition that decisions during this time were collectively reached in a consultative assembly. The caliph only states the consensus reached by the group. For this reason, during this era legislative independent thinking exhibited little disparity, because the jurists were able to compare different narratives in a group meeting and hear all views in one gathering. Such an advantage minimized differences and increased the possibility of attaining a correct decision. For the above reasons, consensus was easily reached during this time period, while it was impossible to attain in later time periods.

Singular *Ijtihād* and Dissent

Once the Companions relocated to different parts of the expanding Islamic world, it became impossible for them to convene before releasing a formal opinion every time an issue was presented. This was not practical or possible given the large size of the Islamic nation, the primitiveness of transportation, and the diversity of issues that people of different ethnicities and different traditions raised.

For these reasons, in each state (*wilāya*) there existed one—or more—scholar who taught the people what he had memorized from the Quran and the Sunna, interpreted legal verses and *aḥādīth*, and issued his own decrees in matters not covered in the Book or the Sunna. In situations where there was more than one scholar in the same state, they met to discuss issues before issuing any formal legal opinion.

Naturally, in these circumstances, disagreements and differences emerged for a number of reasons:

1. The Sunna was not written down.

Thus, it was not available as a standard copy for all legislators. The Sunna at this time was transmitted orally, making it possible for people to report on the authority of Abdullah Ibn Mas`ūd what they did not report on the authority of Abdullah Ibn Umar, or narrate on the authority of Abu Mūsā al- Ash`arī what was not reported on the authority of Mu`ādh Ibn Jabal, and so on.

2. The difference in interpreting legislative verses and legislative *aḥādīth*:

It was possible that one word could mean more than one thing; therefore, interpretation of a text could differ from one scholar to another. For example, in the verse "and the divorced woman shall wait three *qurū'*," the word "*qurū'*" was understood by Umar and Ibn Mas`ūd to mean menstruation, whereas Zayd Ibn Thābit understood it to mean cleanness (*ṭuhr*). As a result, they disagreed regarding the length and timing of the waiting period (*`idda*), whether it was three menstruations or three cleanness periods.

3. The differences and particularities of the environments where these legislators lived:

In other words, the customs and traditions of the people of Kūfa, where Ibn Mas`ūd lived, differed from that of Madīna, the hometown of Abdullah Ibn Umar, or that of Egypt, the residence of Abdullah Ibn Amr Ibn al-`Āṣ, and the same could be said about the environment of Shām where Mu`ādh Ibn Jabal lived. This disparity in environment effected *ijtihād*, given that the purpose of *ijtihād* was to provide for public welfare and prevent any harm or discomfort. Surely, public welfare and comfort differ from one people to another and from one culture to another.

For the above reasons—and other reasons—the *mujtahids'* laws varied from one scholar to another. Any given person from the general public was at liberty to choose anyone's ruling. A Muslim woman, for example, would not hesitate to follow the decree of Ibn Mas`ūd to determine her waiting period, be it three menstrual cycles after her divorce (*qurū'* = menstruation), or three cycles starting from the end of the menstrual period following the divorce as understood by Zayd Ibn Thābit (*qur'* = *ṭuhr*). She might even follow one scholar on one occasion and another scholar on another. It was never made compulsory for people to follow a particular scholar on all of the issues that faced them. If one did follow all of these schools of thought, he would not be misled or committing an error, since all these views stemmed from the *ijtihād* of the Companions, who referred to the same source of legislation and who used analogy. Therefore, none of the scholars deserved to be followed more than the other. It was narrated that Umar Ibn al-Khaṭṭāb once met a man and asked him:

(...) "What have you done?" The man answered: "Zayd has decreed so-and-so for me." `Umar added: "If you asked me I would have decree otherwise." The man asked: "Why don't you do so, are not you the caliph?" `Umar replied: "If I was to order you to follow the Quran and the Sunna I would. But what I said is just my opinion and so was his (just his opinion). So there is no difference."

So far, we have indicated that the Messenger legislated using revelations he received from God and that he added to that body of rulings with his own independent thinking. No one succeeded him and claimed to receive divine revelations. However, a number of scholars inherited his role as independent thinkers (*mujtahid*). Some of his Companions worked to understand the texts. They guided people in the light of their interpretations of the stated laws as well as new laws concerning new issues. Initially, they convened and released opinions that were the product of collective efforts. Later, once these Companions moved to different states, each of them undertook the legislative role along with the scholars who happened to live in the same city where he lived. Later, their students (*tābi`ūn*) followed the same path. Generally speaking, the legislative role was undertaken by a committee, whether the committee was a group of Companions as in the earlier part of this period, or a small group of scholars who lived in the same state later. The limits and domain of their authority was as mentioned previously.

Remarks:

A few things are worth mentioning at this juncture:

1. The Companions paid close attention to the process of writing down the Quran and distributing it in various regions, hence making it a standardized source. During the time of Abu Bakr, for instance, Zayd Ibn Thābit was ordered to collect its loose pages into one single book. (It should be mentioned that during the time of the Messenger, the Quran was written down, but on loose sheets.) For this task, Zayd Ibn Thābit relied on individuals who had memorized the Quran, on collected copies from a number of writers, and on a collection of written Quran passages stored in the house of the Messenger. He verified that with what he himself and other *muhājirūn* and *ansār* memorized to create the first *muṣḥaf*. This collection was kept with Abu Bakr, `Umar, then with Hafṣah Bint Umar—the mother of the believers—until the year 25 after *Hijrah*. At this time (time of the third caliph) Uthmān ordered Zayd Ibn Thābit, Abdullah Ibn al-Zubayr, Sa`d Ibn al-`Āṣ, and Abdul Raḥmān Ibn al-Hārith Ibn Hishām to use this *musḥ*af to publish more copies. Afterwards, he returned the original to Hafṣa, sent copies to the various Islamic states, and kept one copy with himself. These copies were made available in the grand mosques for the general public, for the memorizers, and for legislators. Since the first source of law

was published, no scholar was expected to contradict any part of it under the excuse of not knowing it.

As for the second source of law, the Sunna, the Companions did not record it. In fact, it was reported that they warned against excessively narrating and writing it. Al-Sha`bī reported on the authority of Qaraḍa Ibn Ka`b, who said:

When `Umar ordered us to leave for war in Iraq, he walked with us and asked: "Do you know why I walked with you out of the city?" They replied: "Yes, in our honor." He said: "Besides that, to tell you that you will come on people of a city making noise—while reading the Quran—similar to that of bees. Do not prevent them from that by narrating *ḥadīth* and causing them to occupy themselves by it. Adhere to the Quran and minimize your narration of *ḥadīth*. I will be your partner in that." When Qaraḍa arrived, he was asked: "Tell us (*ḥadīth*)!" He replied: "`Umar has ordered us not to do that."

`Urwah Ibn al-Zubayr reported that when `Umar wanted to write the *Ḥadīth*, he consulted the Prophet's Companions. They approved his suggestion. However, because of some doubt, he chose to wait for a month before taking any action. One day he appeared decisive and addressed the people:

I have mentioned to you my wish to write the Sunna as you may know. But I remembered that some of the People of the Book before you have written—besides the Book of God—other books. Later generations turned to them and left the Book of God. By God, I will not mix the Book of God with anything.' And he decided against writing the Sunna.

Since the Quran was a collected and recorded publication while the Sunna was not—or at least some of it was known to some scholars—it was possible for Abu Bakr, `Umar and others to say that there was no textual proof concerning a particular issue in the Book of God, but a similar statement about the Tradition was not possible. Therefore, they asked people if there was a Tradition from the

Sunna. All the Companions could say was, "I don't know of any Tradition from the Sunna concerning such-and-such issue."

As for the third source of legislation—*ijtihād*—none of the independent thinkers amongst the Companions ever recorded laws resulting from his own *ijtihād*. The caliphs also did not concern themselves with collecting these laws resulting from *ijtihād*. We do not know if they ever recorded these laws, even though the laws were the ijtihād of the collective reached through limited consensus.

In short, they recorded and published the Quran. They thought about writing the Sunna but eventually were limited to simple narration of what they had memorized of it. They did not write their legislative *ijtihād*, and they did not think about doing so because they thought that the foundation of legislation is in the Quran, the prime source that could not be substituted for any other. As for the Sunna, they did not see any harm in its oral transmission as long as the Quran was being recorded and published for the people. Laws resulting from their own independent thinking were taken as extractions (*istinbāṭ*) necessitated by the needs of the people during that time period. These extractions were educed based on their own efforts and their personal understandings of the texts and justifications of laws. They did not consider them to be part of the foundation of legislature emulating the Quran and the Sunna. For this reason, when asked for formal opinions, a scholar would start with a disclaimer indicating that the answer was just his opinion. If correct, then it was from God; if incorrect, then it was from him and from Satan. It was reported that `Umar's secretary wrote: "This is what God and `Umar have decreed." `Umar told him: "Horrible is what you said! This is what `Umar has decreed, if correct, then it is from God; if incorrect then it is from `Umar." Then he added: "The rule is what has been decreed by God and his Messenger. Do not make doubtful opinions rule the *Umma*."

At this point, a number of legitimate questions may be posed:

- Who has talked to the Messenger,

• In whose language was the Quran revealed,

• Who witnessed and learned the "causes of revelations,"

• Who did not consider their decrees and *ijtihād* laws to be followed,

• Who did not write down their decrees, but rather consider them simple personal opinions,

• Who feared that Muslims would occupy themselves with these decrees and take them as alternatives to the Quran and the Sunna,

• What is the cause of what happened later, when the primary source of law for Muslims became the opinions of scholars instead of the Quran? How did the laws resulting from their independent thinking become considered sacred laws, and how did imitating one of the four imāms became compulsory? Why did Islamic governments grow hesitant to adopt a law not mentioned by these *imāms*, although the needs of the people necessitate it and the religious texts do not reject it?

We will study the above points when we present the last period as we continue our discussion of the three branches of the Islamic government.

2. In the course of extracting laws from legislative texts, the people in charge of the legislative branch during this period considered public welfare; they were guided by good nature and determination for truth. When extracting laws, they were restricted by neither regulations nor special interests. With this freedom of thought and with the determination to protect the public interest, Islamic legislation encompassed all the needs of its society during this age. The influence of the Persian empire in Iraq and the Roman empire in Egypt and Shām (Syria, Palestine, and Jordan) caused diversity that resulted in a disparity of needs among Muslims. Despite this, and despite the nomadic character of the people of the Arabian

Peninsula and all those who merged after Islam's expansion, legislators did not hit a hurdle, nor were they short on extracting any law that might support public interest. This is because they found in the book of God and in the Sunna of His Messenger all the texts and rules needed to manage society. They did not find any evidence that would limit their freedom or distract their attention, as long as they did not leave the known boundaries of religion and its general foundations. After this period, however, new rules for *ijtihād* and law-interpretation were put forth. Conditions identifying the need for *ijtihād* were established. These rules and conditions restricted freedom of thought and terminated the protection of many acquired interests (*maṣāliḥ mursala*) for which Sharia did not provide a proof for consideration or dismissal. In this manner, Islamic legislature fell short of adapting to change and it grew incapable of responding to some of the people's needs. Some scholars were aware of these restrictions, so they resorted to providing solutions. For instance, take the statement "the contract is void using analogy, and permitted considering the interests." This statement means that a contract of joint industry or joint agricultural business, for example, is void by analogy (*qiyās*), because the features of the contract do not include the characteristics needed for application in judging the contract, but are permitted considering the public interests as long as there is no harm to anyone else and as long as it does not cause disputes. This consideration of public interest is a hint to the tendency to revert to freedom, which was the pillar of independent thinking in the first period.

3. Legislation during this period was similar to legislation during the time of the Messenger, since it was legislation dealing with newly developed matters and it was meant to accommodate the needs of the people. In other words, the scholars among the Companions did not theorize on hypothetical cases and issues and propose answers. Rather, they limited themselves to basic needs. The legislators did not waste their time in the legislature as "professional law makers," especially since they were in charge of other affairs of the state. They only gave formal opinions once someone approached them for that purpose. Because of that, laws resulting

from the Companions' independent thinking were fewer than those recorded from the later period.

4. Disparity was a result of different interpretations of texts by Companion scholars from a linguistic viewpoint as well as the possibility that a *Ḥadīth* could be known to one Companion and unknown to another. Scholars might have different viewpoints on the reasons behind a particular law. Divergent analyses and determinations of the peoples' needs could have aggravated this disparity. Political affiliations, tendencies of the caliph, or blind support of a particular viewpoint resulting from subservience of scholars to political leaders did not influence the scholars' decisions at this stage. Such reality minimized or limited a divergence of trends in legislature during this period. In fact, it was common practice that one of these early scholars reversed his decision once another opinion prevailed or if he came to learn about a new Tradition from the Messenger.

The Judiciary and the Judges

We have said that during the time of the Messenger [PBUH], it was he who served as judge in person; he also delegated that authority to his governors and designated special counsel to settle specific disputes. He never appointed a judge to serve as a judge and only as a judge in any of the Islamic states, because there was no need for such an action, as we have explained. After his demise and during the early days of Abu Bakr's caliphate, judicial power was encompassed within the caliphate. This is because the caliphate was regarded as a succession (*khilāfa*) to the ultimate legislative authority, and the caliph was expected to continue inviting non-Muslims to this religion, protecting as well as to governing and organizing the affairs of the people according to God's words. This type of succession, then, necessitated that the caliph hold judicial power. The caliph needed to be able to serve on any post that helped him to run the affairs of Muslims, even if that meant consolidating legislative, judicial, and executive powers.

The caliph served in the judicial post. He sometimes delegated this authority to others. During Abu Bakr's caliphate and the first part of `Umar's, the judiciary post was run the same way it had been operating during the time of the Messenger, because Abu Bakr was particularly uncomfortable with making changes to a procedure or law inherited from the Messenger. In addition, there were not that many happenings requiring a policy change during this period. Evidently, Abu Bakr, who served as a judge in the case of the grandmother when he ruled for her to inherit the sixth, was using the same procedure adopted by the Prophet. He used the Quran and his knowledge of Sunna, as mentioned in the Tradition we cited above. It was reported that when a dispute was brought before `Umar and he did not find a ruling concerning it in the Book or in the Sunna, he asked if Abu Bakr had issued a ruling in a similar case. In other instances, he sought the help of prominent Companions before making a ruling. It was narrated that when he was appointed first caliph, Abu `Ubaydah told him: "I will lift the burden of treasury from you" and `Umar told him: "I will lift the burden of judiciary from you." He also delegated judicial power to his governors. It was reported that the governors of Abu Bakr used to rule on disputed matters or appoint trusted individuals to help them in judicial affairs. This was the case also during the time of the Messenger.

Once `Umar was in charge, he preserved the same judicial structure set up by the Messenger and maintained by Abu Bakr until the expansion of the Islamic land. At this time, the interests of the state became more complex and the responsibilities of the governors augmented. The caliph alone was no longer able to retain the judicial branch. The same can be said about governors in some of the other states. In the middle of his caliphate, `Umar started a process of separation and decentralization. He delegated judicial affairs to judges. For instance, he appointed Abu al-Dardā' as judge in Madīna, Sharīḥ judge in Kūfa, and Abu Mūsā al- Ash`arī judge of Baṣra. In this context, Ibn al-Zahrī and Ibn Musīb commented:

Neither the Messenger of God nor Abu Bakr had ever designated judges. It was `Umar who asked Ali to take part of the new responsibilities from him some times in the middle of his caliphate.

It was at this point of history that judges began running the judicial branch. The caliph himself mainly appointed these judges. `Umar Ibn al-Khaṭṭāb first appointed Sharīḥ as a judge in Kūfa, whom he later established as the permanent judge there. Sharīh stayed serving in that position for about seventy-five years—until the time of Abdul Malik Ibn Marwān. On other occasions, it was the governors who appointed judges. `Amr Ibn al-`Āṣ, then-governor of Egypt, designated Uthmān Ibn al-Qays Ibn Abu al-`Āṣ judge in the same state. However, the governors appointed judges only in the states they governed as determined by the caliph, who had the authority to appoint judges or delegate that authority to his governors to designate judges. It was reported that when Caliph Ali appointed al-Ashtar al-Nakh`ī as governor of Egypt, he wrote to him saying:

> ... And choose a judge amongst the best of your constituents, one who does not grow tired of serving, nor who is bothered by disputes. One who does not persist erring, nor who shies from returning to the truth once he knows it. One who fears corruption and seeks the maximum understanding instead of the minimum, one amongst them who ponders most on confusion and takes seriously evidence, one who is least uncomfortable with attempting to reconcile between the plaintiffs and the defendants, one who is most patient in unveiling the matters, one who is strict and sure once he sees the ruling and is not doubtful, one who is hard to bribe. And know that they are very few.

Al-Ashtar was killed before he reached Egypt and this document that contained the foundation of judicial policies did not materialize.

The act of appointing judges did not prevent the caliph from serving as judge, since the appointed judge was considered his helper. `Umar, for instance, settled disputes amongst the citizens of Madīna, although he had already appointed Abu al-Baṣra judge of Madīna. All of the other righteously guided caliphs did the same on occasion. As for the governors, I did not read any materials indicating, one way or another, that they participated along with their appointed judges. It appears, however, that the governors who were permitted to appoint judges held themselves judicial authority as well as the power to appoint judges.

References Used by Judges

Judges at this stage were *mujtahids*. They solely referred to the Book and the Sunna. If they found rulings in these two sources they used them. Otherwise, they ruled using their own ijtihād. Since the Book was already written down and published so that readers, judges, and muftīs could use it, it was easy for them to determine if a text dealing with a particular dispute at hand existed or not. But because the Sunna was not recorded and published, it was not as simple for a judge alone to determine whether the Messenger of God had ruled in a similar case. For that reason, the judge must consult the learned Companions and scholars in his state to know if there was a Tradition from the Messenger. In the case that he did not learn of any Tradition, he would strive to make his ruling independently. But in most cases, the ruling was stated after deliberation with the council of consultation (*shūra*). This approach was evident from what we have previously explained regarding Abu Bakr's and `Umar's process of consultation with prominent scholars and Companions in the absence of legislative verses and legislative Traditions. When asking if there were Traditions, they would make the announcement public since anyone at that time could have heard a saying from the Messenger. For consultation, however, only prominent Companions and scholars convened, since not all people were capable of issuing a formal opinion or exerting independent thinking. The rest of the righteously guided caliphs and the appointed governors and judges followed the same path. The judges regularly contacted the legislature, so making laws was the result of a consultative process. In each state, individuals who had memorized the Quran and Traditions served as advisors or consultants to the judge in charge. The fact that the judges referred to these scholars was not understood as imitation—since they were all *mujtahids*—rather, it was an effort to see whether they knew of a Tradition or an opinion that was unavailable to him, so that his ruling did not contradict the Sunna. Collective *ijtihād* was believed to increase the probability of reaching a correct decision. For the same reason, judges consistently consulted with the caliph before ruling on certain issues, because the caliph had many prominent scholars around him as advisors whose opinions might be closer to the truth.

Despite the fact that the sources of law that legislators referred to at this time were the Quran, the Sunna, or the *ijtihād* of the consultative councils, the rulings were not recorded as later guidelines or precedent; the shared belief then was to not force anyone to follow anything but the Quran and the Sunna. This also enabled the judges and the scholars to use only these two sources. If one were to read the history of the life of Sharīh, al- Sha`bī, Iyās, Uthmān Ibn Qays, or other judges, he would find very little information regarding the rulings they issued. Whatever little happened to be recorded was intended to express the degree of their maturity in the field of law, or to comment on opinions in specific cases. The same way the *mujtahids* were free, judges were also unbound by any rules except general guidelines in the Quran and the Sunna. Judges not only performed *ijtihād* on subject matters, but also performed *ijtihād* on the procedures in their courts, like requiring proof from plaintiffs and oaths if defendants denied. It was their custom not to rule unless they heard both sides. They showed great commitment to establishing justice, using all necessary means including requiring proofs, oaths, evidence, and even intuition. That is because it was wiser to use all possible means to reach truth and justice than to close the doors in the face of any attempt. For those interested in learning about the freedom of judges and the procedures used at that time, they may read the book: al-Turuq al-Ḥakīma fī al-Siyāsa al-Shar`iyya, by Ibn al-Qayyim (d.751 H.).

Specialization and Jurisdiction of Judges

Subjective specialization (*ikhtiṣāṣ*), which refers to the kinds of disputes or issues that constitute a judge's area of specialty, was never present at this period of time. We know, for example, that `Umar appointed Abu al-Baṣra as judge in Egypt, but we don't know whether he restricted him to an area of law. Historical documents, however, reflect that judges at this stage ruled in civil disputes as well as family matters. This is evident from the materials presented Ibn al-Qayyim's book mentioned above. The subjects presented include disputed due loans, claims of wife or child support, and other matters that can be classified as civil claims or civil penal codes.

Professor al-Khiḍrī Bic, may God's mercy be upon him, said in his lectures titled "*Tārīkh al-umam al-islāmiyya*" (the history of the Islamic nation) on page 458:

It appears to us that the rulings of the judges during the time of the first four caliphs were limited to civil disputes. Private claims (*qiṣāṣ*) and public offenses (*ḥūdūd*) were under the jurisdiction of the caliph and governors. We know that the caliphs and *amīrs* ruled in matters of murder or flogging the drunker, but we did not hear of any judge who is not a governor and who ruled in these matters or even participated in the execution of laws of this area. Correctional penalties like prison cannot be ordered, save by the caliph or his agents. So, the jurisdiction of judges was very limited.

In Egypt, also, Mu`āwiyya once ordered the judge, Salīm Ibn `Iṭr, to rule in civil disputes.

We can then conclude that judicial power was a partnership between judges and governors who specialized in grievances (*maẓālim*). Grievance, as explained by al-Māwardī in his book *al-Aḥkām al-sulṭāniyya*, as:

> (...) forcing aggressors to act justly using force, warning the disputing individuals to settle their disputes using authority.
>
> Ibn Khaldūn defined it as:
>
> governance as an imbuement of the power of the king and the fairness of the judge. It needs an upper hand and great fear that can end aggression in disputes and warn the aggressor. The serving agent has to look at the evidence and reports, analyze all the proofs and evidence, delay the ruling until the truth is clear, and force the accused to reconcile before witnesses. These duties are beyond the judge.
>
> Al-Māwardī continued in his book, saying:

None of the four caliphs ever appointed judges, because at this early stage of the life of the Islamic community, people were deterred from persisting in committing aggression through truth and the concept of justice as moral values. Most disputes were a result of discrepancies that needed to be explained by law. As for the rough nomads, warnings were enough to deter them from committing any aggression. Thus the caliphs settled disputes where there was a need to explain or state the law. However, during his late caliphate, Ali [RAA] was forced to introduce stricter laws and pay more attention to the particulars of cases. He was the first one to introduce changes in the legal system and not restrict his duties to rule in disputes. Because of this increased scope of responsibilities... and when aggression became rampant and warnings failed to serve as a deterrent, a system combining the power of the authority and the justice of the judicial process became needed to stop aggressors and protect the oppressed. The first ruler to reserve one day to hear disputes without being personally involved in the hearing was Abdul Malik Ibn Marwān. He appointed Judge Abu Idrīs al-'Awdī to execute the laws. Therefore, Abu Idrīs was the immediate Executive Judge while Abdul Malik served as the Ordering (or substantive) one.

What can be concluded from the history of judicial power during this period is that judges were similar to muftīs. Their rulings were similar to decrees, as explained in the quote from Abu al-Ḥasan al-Māwardī:

> (...) Disputes were more like inquiries regarding vague issues, about which a person was not sure of the view of the new religion, hence the ruling of the judges were sought simply for clarification.

If a dispute was not a matter as described above, but rather a case of aggression, then, it was the grievances' agents who would rule. Since people willingly brought their cases before judges, it was not necessary to keep records of cases where the ruling was written down as reference for the aggrieved side. Once the number of disputes increased and denials started to appear, judges were compelled to record their rulings. The first judge to do so was the judge of Egypt, Salīm Ibn `Eṭr, who was appointed by Mu`āwiyya.

As for locale (geographic jurisdiction), it can be concluded from the written documents that judges were appointed to the whole state, the same way a governor was appointed to govern the entire state. The judges could also select helpers and assistants as needed, the same way a governor did.

Evidently, if we read the history of the judicial branch in Egypt or Syria, we would not find any indication of the existence of more than one judge in a single state. So we can conclude that one judge indeed served the whole state. This could be the result of the participation of the governors and caliphs in the settlement of legal disputes, thus causing the number of cases requiring a judge's legal intervention to be very limited. In other words, each state did not need more than one judge to clarify ambiguous situations. Judges' activities were conducted in the mosques with few exceptions during the time of `Uthmān, who introduced courthouses.

Remarks

A few important matters concerning the judicial power may be noted here:

1. There was absolute freedom enjoyed by the judge as he made rulings or as he chose the procedure through which he reached the rulings. It was never the case where a judge was limited to decree according to a particular school of thought or according to a particular *mujtahid's* view. Procedure was not predetermined for him. Since all the rulings were based on *ijtihād*, judges could state different rulings in similar cases without voiding a prior ruling or voiding the ruling of another judge. This was the case in the Tradition reported on `Umar who was told that Ali and Zayd ruled such-and-such, to which he replied that he would have ruled differently if he were the judge. It was also narrated that he ruled with one ruling in one case, then, later, he issued a different ruling in a similar case. When asked about this inconsistency he said: "That was my ruling then, and this is my ruling now." This was possible because his ruling stemmed from *ijtihād*. As long as the rulings were based on the same principles, there was no need for them to cancel one another out, because *ijtihād* in both cases was susceptible to error. That being the case, now we can understand why there was no court of appeals during this period.

2. Judges were not limited to a particular field of law, nor did they specialize in a particular area. This character did not have any negative impact on the judges, because the caliphs and the governors at this early stage respected them and did not question their qualifications. When a case was brought before Abdul Malik, for example, he referred it to his judge Abu Idrīs. The judge was then the executive judge, while the caliph served as the ultimate judge. Not defining the specialty area of the judges at this time caused the loss of most of their rights later. The judicial branch became a partnership between powerful governors—who selected what they

wanted—and weak judges who were restricted to sit on cases that politicians deemed unimportant. The responsibilities of judges increased and decreased depending on the wishes and whims of the governors.

3. There was no written or pronounced document requiring governors to enforce judges' rulings. This was not a factor in the early period, because the rulings were in the form of formal opinions that people themselves willingly sought. Hence, there was no need to enforce the judges' orders. With the initiation of the post, judges needed executive powers to enforce the law. This power was in the hands of governors who were not bound by a higher decree or executive order requiring them to carry out the judges' decisions. In fact, it was left to a governor to execute any ruling they wished and ignore those that they wanted to ignore. This element reduced the authority of the judicial system in the eyes of the public. People then preferred the amirs and governors to settle their disputes instead of judges. For this reason, a judge's order's enforceability was dependent on his relationship with the governor; that is to say, that if a judge was supported by the governor, people would abide by his rulings. If not, his rulings would be regarded as non-binding decrees.

4. Some of the judges carried out the executions of their orders themselves. These judges, especially Ali and Sharīḥ, had the power to execute the laws they stated. This, however, was not common practice, because most people willingly executed the laws.

A Selection of Rulings from this Period

Below, we introduce a selection of rulings from the most famous judges of this period. It gives a clear picture of the organization of the judicial branch. These famous cases were reported by Ibn Qayyim al-Jawziyya in the book al-Turuq *al-ḥakīma fī al-siyāsa al-Shar`iyya.*

It was reported on the authority of al- Sha`bī that al-Muqdād had borrowed seven thousand *dirhams* from Uthmān. He then returned only four thousand. Uthmān reminded him that it was seven thousand *dirhams*, but al-Muqdād insisted that he borrowed only four thousand *dirhams*. The dispute, then, was brought before `Umar. al-Muqdād said:

"O! Commander of the Faithful, ask him to swear that it is as he says, then I will let him have what he says."

`Umar commented:

"He is fair with you; do swear that it is that much and it will be yours."

From Ali's rulings, we report that an orphan female was living with a married man who stayed away from home most of the time. When the orphan grew up, the wife feared that her husband would marry her. She called some of her neighbors, who helped her hold the girl while she broke her virginity with her finger. When her husband returned home, the wife accused the girl of fornication and took her claim before Ali. Ali asked if she had any witnesses. She replied that her neighbors would testify to this effect. Ali sent for them. When they came in, he sent them to separate rooms and put his sword before him then called the wife, who insisted that she was telling the truth and urged him to consider her claim. He sent her to the room and called one of the witnesses. Once before him, Ali set on his knees and said:

"The woman said what she said but now she told the truth and I gave her my word that she will not be harmed. If you do not say the truth I will do so-and-so to you."

The witness said:

"No, by God she (the girl) did not do anything. The wife saw in the girl some seductive beauty and she feared that she would lose her husband, so she called us to help her do what she did."

Ali then said:

"God is Great! I was the first to separate between the two witnesses."

Then he ruled that the wife be penalized for slander (*qadhf*). As for the women, he forgave them all. He also ordered the man to divorce his wife and marry the orphan and he paid the dowry on the husband's behalf.

It was reported that two women brought a case before Ka`b Ibn Sūr, the judge appointed by `Umar. Each of the two women had a child but one of them fell on one of the children and killed him. So each one of them claimed that the living child was hers. Ka`b said: "I'm not Sulaymān Ibn Dawūd," then ordered someone to bring him some fresh soil, which he spread on the ground; then, he ordered each of the women to walk on it. After that he asked the child to walk on the same dirt. Finally, he asked a track trailer to look at the footprints and decide to whom the child belonged.

A man loaned money to another, who later denied borrowing money from him. The case was presented before Iyās Ibn Mu`āwiyya. Iyās asked the plaintiff: "Where did you give him the money?" He answered: "In the wilderness." Iyās continued: "What was there?" The plaintiff replied: "A tree." Iyās then said: "Go back there and look around the tree; maybe you have buried the money under it and forgot. Maybe when you see the tree you will remember." While the man was on his way the defendant remained in the courtroom as the judge continued hearing the rest of the cases. After a while he asked him: "Do you think that your friend reached the tree now?" The defendant answered: "No!" The judge then said: "You are a cheater, O! You enemy of God." The defendant then begged for mercy but the judge ordered him to be handed over to the plaintiff when he came back, who would go with him to get his money.

I will conclude the presentation of these examples by mentioning what Ibn al-Qayyim reported in *al-Turuq al-ḥakīma*:

A man asked Iyās Ibn Mu`āwiyya to teach him judgeship. He answered that it cannot be taught, for it is an intellectual matter.

But if you ask me to teach you the science which is the heart of the matter, in that regard God has said: "And Dawūd and Sulaymān who have ruled in the case of the field used by some people's sheep. We were witnesses of their ruling, which we have made clear for Sulaymān and for both of them we have given wisdom and knowledge." So, He has privileged Sulaymān with the understanding of the case and made the knowledge of it attainable by the public.

`Umar wrote to his judge, Abu Mūsā, stressing the importance of understanding that which is stated in each given case. It is true that Iyās and Sharīḥ were educated men who had acquired a great deal of knowledge in this discipline; however, they also showed a good understanding of the cases and as they relied on signs and witnesses. Governors who lacked these characteristics made bad judges and issued many erroneous judicial orders that caused the loss of rights and denied victims due legal remedies.

Executive Power during this Period

We earlier defined executive matters of the Islamic state as the various actions and decisions undertaken by the caliph, the governors, and the other agents of the state required to run the affairs of the *Umma* besides the legislative and judicial affairs. Some researchers defined them as "administrative measures." They were all of the things which were required by different sectors of the government including financial, educational, military, agricultural, and economic matters. They were also necessary executive actions undertaken by the caliph or governors regarding appointments, removal, and supervision of other administrators. These executive orders extended to determine the job requirements and jurisdictions of these appointed agents. Executive matters also referred to relations between different governing institutions as well as the relationship of governorships (appointed governors) with the leadership (caliphate). In general terms, they included all actions—besides legislation and judiciary—the governing body undertook in order to preserve the interests of the nation and to secure the safety of groups and individuals inside or outside the country.

There is no doubt that examining administrative business of the Islamic state throughout different periods and pondering on its nature as well as its changes is very hard for the researcher to attain. This is due to the fact that this business is not solely of a religious nature that can be extracted from texts of the sources of Islamic laws. It is also due to the diversity of these laws in different states, since each state had its own administrative organization that was compatible with the customs and the needs of its people. Very few historians have occupied themselves with detailing the administrative organization of each state, followed their evolutions, and recorded the differences between the organization of the executive offices in one state or another. Today, we find only fragments here and there recorded along with the Sīra of the caliphs and governors. Mohammed al-Khidrī Bic recorded most of it in his book *Tārīkh al-umam al-islāmiyya*. Professor Mohammed Kurd Ali also collected some of these issues in his book *al-Idāra al-Islāmiyya fī `izz al-`arab* (Islamic Administration during the Golden ages of the Arabs), and so did Mr. al-Katānī in his books *al-Tarātīb al-idāriyya* and *Niḍām al-ḥukūma al-nabawiyya.*

At this juncture, we will enlist the general foundation on which stands the administration of the Islamic state during this period. Then we will proceed to detail some of the manifestations of administrative work, hoping that these examples from executive affairs, along with what we have presented concerning legislation and judiciary, together can create a clearer picture of the policies of the Islamic government during the time of the Companions.

First principle: The Consolidation of Power

The executive administration hinged on the authority of the caliphate and the power of the caliph. It was perceived as such, not only because the caliph was the leader of the Islamic state who inherited the responsibility of protecting the religion as well as the policies in this world through the process of *bay`a* (allegiance), but also because he enjoyed the right to claim control over all operations of the state and execute any order he deemed necessary for materializing that which he promised the people during his election (selection). But since he could not perform all this work by himself, he was obliged to appoint governors and agents who would act on his behalf in certain matters as necessitated by circumstance. In other words, all of the bureaucrats of the state were his deputies, acting on his behalf. He had the power to appoint them, discharge them, and supervise them. Generally, he also determined the authority of the governor and its boundaries. The caliph then enjoyed supreme power and supreme authority. It was possible that a caliph appointed a governor and increased his duties to include choosing the agents and other public servants. This was the case when `Amr Ibn al-`Āṣ was appointed governor of Egypt and Mu`āwiyya appointed governor of Syria. It was also possible for the caliph to appoint a governor and someone else as a special agent to collect taxes and alms; hence, for each of them a special duty. For example, along with `Ammār Ibn Yāsir, who was appointed governor of Iraq, Abdullah Ibn Mas`ūd also was appointed to teach the Quran and supervise finances. `Umar wrote to the people of Iraq when `Ammār Ibn Yāsir was governor, saying:

> I have put in charge of your treasury Abdullah Ibn Mas`ūd and I have chosen him for you over myself.

The decision to increase the power of one governor and limit that of another, offering more freedom for one and restricting that of another, depended on how much the caliph trusted the appointee and his assessment of the public interest if governed by one person or another. This conscious selectivity stemmed from his awareness that these duties and responsibilities were actually his, thus he had the right to choose the individual who represented him best.

Nothing limited his power in this respect except public welfare. This absolute power was positive when the caliph cared only to serve the public, thus using this power justly in order to materialize public interest. The negative side of this structure, however, emerged once the priorities of the caliph changed when he prioritized acquiring more power and securing the support of particular ethnic and social classes. Such an approach was adopted even if it jeopardized the public welfare.

Second Principle: *shūra*

The righteously guided caliphs did not turn the process of governing into a monarchy. They always consulted people of opinion amongst the Companions. Abu Bakr, for instance, used to convene with the *muhājirīn* and the *anṣ*ār, and so did `Umar and the rest of the Rāshid caliphs after him. There are many documents describing the consultative council gathered by Abu Bakr before deciding on the war of apostasy as well as the council `Umar established to discuss taxes assessed on the use of the public lands (*arḍ al-sawād*). One can easily notice the freedom enjoyed by individuals who served on these councils in expressing their opinions and stating their arguments. These features provide us with a fair assessment of the level of attention awarded to shūra.

Professor al-Khidrī Bic—may God's mercy be with him—wrote in his book *Tārīkh al-umam al-Islāmiyya,* on page 354 vol. 3:

If a matter is brought before `Umar, he does not decide on it until he gathers Muslims and consults them about it. He used to say: "There is no good in an individual who decides without consultation." His consultation was of different degrees; he used to consult the public first, then he gathered the elders among the Companions of Quraysh and others. Whenever they agreed on one view he took it. He said in this regard: "It is the right of Muslims to see the people of opinion amongst them being consulted."

In Vol. 3, page 454 we read:

> `Umar had a private council formed out of prominent Companions like Uthmān, al-Abbās, Ali Ibn Abī Ṭālib, and Abdul Raḥmān Ibn `Awf. He also had a general council made of all individuals of opinions amongst the Muslims. He used to present the issue in the mosque after he called for prayer, and then state what he wanted, and finally he consulted his private advisors.

The same way judicial and legislative branches brought about justice and truth, the consultative process limited the absolute power of the caliph and moderated administrative affairs. But a law obliging the caliph to adopt a consultative government was never institutionalized as a way of preventing him from transforming the caliphate into a monarchy. Even the verses "And consult them in their affairs" (*wa shāwirhum fī al-amr*), and God's statement that the way Muslims ought to run their affairs "shall be decided through consultation amongst them" (*wa amruhum shūrā baynahum*), were not taken as commands to establish consultative councils, nor were they taken to oblige the ruler to adopt the decision of consultative assemblies. This was because some of the scholars—may God forgive them—decreed that the above commands of establishing *shūra* were of the "preferred" (*mandūb*) category, not the obligatory one (*wujūb*). Other scholars, who said that those verses were commands of obligation, added that the advised individual is not obliged to be limited by the decisions of his advisor or of the council. In the light of these interpretations, some of the caliphs destroyed the institution of the *shūra* and used their absolute power to do whatever they wanted, to the extent that Abdullah Ibn Marwān said: "Whoever tells me "fear God" (*ittaqī Allāh*) after this moment, I shall cut his neck." This attitude came to replace that of `Umar, who declared: "Whoever sees me doing something wrong, he must correct me."

There were no established standards determining the qualifications of individuals needed to serve on consultative councils. In fact, the caliph was free to appoint members of such councils, factor in their recommendations, or do away with the entire process all together without any restrictions. He did not have to consult them at all if he did not want to. It was a trend that the Rāshidūn caliphs consulted those who could provide guidance for them, whereas the non-Rāshidūn caliphs consulted only their inner circles of confidants.

Third Principle: Decentralized Government

During the period of the Rāshidūn caliphs and in the early part of the Umayyad Caliphate, governors enjoyed absolute freedom. They ran the affairs of their state however they wanted. In some instances, they cherry-picked issues to report to the caliph. There was no central government per se at this stage. Each state was an independent entity. `Amr Ibn al-`Āṣ in Egypt, Mu`āwiyya in Shām, and Sa``d Ibn Abī Waqqās in Iraq all were independent governors running their respective states as they wanted and as they deemed necessary in order to materialize public interest under the supervision of the caliph. But this kind of arrangement was dictated by the caliph and not by written laws. For this reason, when some of the caliphs sought to centralize the government and consolidate more power in their hands, they limited the governors' powers and prohibited governors from undertaking certain decisions unless they sought prior clearance from them. Al-Ḥajjāj Ibn Yūsuf, for example, was the absolute ruler in Iraq during the caliphate of Abdul Malik Ibn Marwān. He killed, imprisoned, and flogged for any kind of sin. Neither the caliph nor anyone else objected to that. During the time of Sulaymān Ibn Abdul Malik, his power was limited. During the time of `Umar Ibn Abdul `Azīz, once he saw the corruption running rampant among governors who have absolute freedom, he deprived them of this freedom and mandated that any execution of capital punishment laws (killing, flogging, or cutting hands) must be brought to his attention for his personal approval first.

Fourth principle: Qualifications

Governors and agents were selected carefully during the early part of this period. Only qualified individuals were offered such posts. The selection was never based on special personal favors, nor meant to please particular people. This process was established by the Messenger [PBUH] through his deeds and sayings; he appointed individuals from the Umayyad clan to three-fourths of the positions, although many Hashimites were qualified to a certain extent to hold such positions. When Abu Dharr, for example, asked him for a governor's position, he turned him down saying: "O! Abu Dharr, you are a weak man. What you are asking for is a trust." When the *Ash`arī* asked for the same thing he replied: "By God I do not appoint for this job someone who asks for it nor someone who insists on having it." It was reported that he said: "Whoever puts a man in charge of the affairs of a group knowing that there is in the group another man who is better qualified than him, he has betrayed God, His Messenger, and the believers."

The early caliphs who appointed only qualified individuals adopted this principle. The caliphs then were looking for physically able leaders who also possessed strong moral character. As a result, the administrators of state operations at this early stage were efficient and trouble-free. `Umar was exceptionally good at selecting agents; he prolonged consultation and discussion of the matter before he appointed agents. If it happened that he appointed one, and then later found someone else who was more qualified, he discharged the first and replaced him with the second. Despite the distance separating him from his governors, he was well aware of the way they ran their respective states. He made it a habit to ask any visitor, and open his door to any individual with a grievance. He drew up very strict policies that enabled him to supervise the governors and check the sources of their wealth. These policies strengthened the Islamic state and instilled an atmosphere of order in the public life and effectiveness of administration. Once they moved from this path—the family of Uthmān started appointing agents and individuals on the basis of tribal affiliation and personal favors—the authority of the central government deteriorated and civil wars were ignited. We have discussed this issue in our lecture titled: "al-Muwaẓafūn fī sadr al-dawlah al-Islāmiyya," which was published in the second issue in the second year of *al-Muwaẓẓaf* magazine.

In short, this was the principle the Companions adopted to administer public affairs. During this period they managed to govern successfully, which permitted the expansion of the boundaries of the Islamic state. The people of Africa, Egypt, Syria, and Iraq saw justice and fairness in the hands of these Bedouin that they had not seen when they were governed by the Persians or the Romans.

As examples, we mention the administration of the treasury, the administration of the military, and finally the organization of the executive branch during this period.

The Treasury

We have already said that during the time of the Messenger of God, Muslims did not have a treasury because the revenues of the state were very little compared to its expenses.

Zakā and other kinds of alms were spent as determined by God: "As for alms, they are for the poor... (Mentioning the eight beneficiaries from this type of revenues)."

Ghanā'im were spent also as determined by God: "And know that whatever you have captured, for God the fifth ..."

al-Fee': "What God Has granted to His Messenger from the people of the cities ..."

The rest of revenues were spent on general needs of the state, as we have explained in the section about financial policies in our book: *al-Siyāsa al-shar`iyya*. At this time, revenues were spent the same day they reached the Prophet's hands. If there was anything left, the Messenger stored it in his house and in the houses of the Companions.

During the time of Abu Bakr, if any revenues reached Madīna from another state, he took them to the mosque and distributed them as determined above. Later, he established a treasury house in the suburbs of Madīna, but rarely was money stored in it, because revenues during this time did not grow above that during the time of the Messenger. In fact, Abu Bakr followed the procedure of the Messenger in this area like he did in all areas. It was reported that after his demise, `Umar and a few other Companions went to this house to account for the money, but they did not find anything.

During the time of `Umar, however, and with the expansion of the Islamic state and the increase in revenues, `Umar established *Dīwān al-kharāj* in order to organize the treasury of the state and to balance the budget.

The word *dīwān* originally meant the place where the money circulates in and out in form of revenues and expenses. Later, it referred to the special written documents and the posts occupied by individuals in charge of the treasury.

Kharāj originally refers to the name of what is due as taxes on the land where non-Muslims reside, hence the name *al-arḍ al-kharājiyya.* Later, it was generalized to refer to all the state revenue. And, finally, it was used to mean the financial organization, including its revenues and the expenses. For those interested in this this field, we ought to mention the book *al-kharāj* by Judge Abu Yūsuf, written for Caliph Hārūn al-Rashīd, which is considered to be the best Islamic by-laws on finances.

It was said that Umar decided to initiate *Dīwān al-kharāj* after receiving a sum of five hundred thousand dirhams from his agent in Baḥrayn, which he kept guarded in the mosque fearing that it might be stolen. Some people familiar with Persia and Shām suggested that he create the *Dīwān* and he did. *Dīwān al-kharāj* of Madīna was maintained in Arabic and the people in charge of it were from Quraysh. *Dīwān al-kharāj* in Shām was in Latin, the one in Iraq was in Persian, and the one in Egypt was in Coptic; and the agents working on them respectively were Christians, Zoroastrians, and Christians, not Muslims, since Muslims did not know the language of dīwān or the method of calculations used. The various *dawāwīn* remained in their original languages until the Arabs mastered these languages, then they translated them into Arabic. The *dīwān* of Iraq was translated from Persian by Sālah Ibn Abdul Raḥmān during the caliphate of Abdul Malik Ibn Marwān and the governorship of al-Hajjāj. The *dīwān* of Egypt was translated from Coptic by Yarbū` al-Fazarī in 87 H. during the caliphate of al-Walīd Ibn Abdul Malik and the governorship of Abdullah Ibn Abdul Malik. The *dīwān* of Shām was translated from Latin by Abu Thābit Sulaymān Ibn Sa`d during the caliphate of al-Walīd Ibn Abdul Mālik. After that, all records were kept in the Arabic language in all Islamic states.

At this time, state finances were organized so that each state had its own independent budget. In other words, all the revenue of each state was spent within it; the remainder was sent to the caliph to be spent on affairs related to all states. Some revenue was saved for emergencies. This information on expenses was reported in the book titled *al-Khuṭaṭ* by al-Maqrīzī, who reported that `Amr Ibn al-`Āṣ sent money to `Umar after he kept what he needed for the state of Egypt. It was reported that `Amr did not send him anything for some years. `Umar then wrote to him:

"I have thought about your situation and how you are doing, and I realized that your land is large and fertile. God has given its people the manpower, the animals, and power in the land and in the sea. The pharaohs did well despite their arrogance and their disbelief. It amazes me that you have not sent me even half of what you used to provide when there was drought."

`Amr replied:

"I worked during the time of the Messenger and during the time of those who succeeded him and we were—praises be to God—

fulfilling the trust, protecting the rights of the community that God valued. We believed that doing otherwise was wrong. God has purified us from the sinful morsels so that we do not even think of it."

`Umar wrote, answering:

"I did not send you to Egypt to find a morsel of food for yourself, nor for your family. But I chose you for what I hoped to be in your character: save the revenue and govern fairly and justly. Once you receive this book, send me the *kharāj*, which is the right of Muslims. As you may know I have people in great need."

`Amr replied:

"The people of this land asked me to wait until their fruits were ready. So, I did, because I did not want Muslims of this land to be forced to sell what they would not sell otherwise."

From this correspondence, we can clearly see the governors' degree of independence during this time. Each state had the option of saving for emergencies. Their net revenue was not all shipped to Ḥijāz. Rather, a portion was stored in the treasuries of Syria, Egypt, and Iraq. Military personnel and other servants were paid directly from this revenue.

The best feature of the financial administration during this period was that it did not exceed the legal Islamic boundaries of revenue; Muslims and non-Muslims (*dhimmīs*) were not asked to pay except that which was commanded in the Islamic doctrines like *zakāt*, *`ushr* (tenth), *jizyah*, and land taxes. The taxed wealth was determined according to the principles of justice and equality. `Umar once told two of his tax agents in Iraq: "Maybe you overtaxed people to a level that they cannot bear?" One of them replied: "I left behind most of it." The second agent said: "I left behind half of it." `Umar commented: "By God, if it was left for the widows of the people of Iraq, I will let them have it so that they will not beg another leader after me." `Amr Ibn al-`Āṣ also accepted the harshness and criticism of `Umar instead of disregarding the needs of his people in Egypt.

Generally speaking, during this period justice and equality prevailed; no public interest was ever ignored and no rights were lost. The importance they gave to the treasury reached the point where the caliphs appointed ministers to run it in some states instead of the governor. These individuals were generally among the best Companions. For instance, `Umar appointed Abdullah Ibn Mas`ūd to the treasury of Iraq. Other caliphs appointed one special agent in charge of alms and another in charge of *kharāj*. The agents were closely watched by both the caliph and the governor. They stressed accountability and listened to all the complaints related to these agents. A proof of the successful management of the treasury during this period is the noticeable increase in revenues, the establishment of numerous public facilities, and the rise in net revenues in the treasure houses. The book *al-Kharāj* by Abu Yūsuf contains data that supports these conclusions.

The Military

The commander-in-chief of the Muslim armies was the Messenger of God and, after him, his successors. The Messenger of God led armies in person during the twenty-six *gazwahs*. The rest of his *sarāyā* were under the command of some of his Companions. However, the caliphs rarely led their armies. Ali Ibn Abī Ṭālib commanded the army in some battles. The caliphs did not generally lead military missions because the Islamic state expanded its control over larger areas, thus making it hard for the caliph to leave Madīna for wars. Instead, the caliphs selected individuals with military skill and courage to replace them. It should also be noted that during the time of the Messenger and during the caliphate of Abu Bakr, all Muslims were considered soldiers, expected to serve and defend their community and Islamic ideals. There was not a group of them professionally trained and reserved for war. Troops did not receive a determined pension from the treasury, either, but they did share war revenues in a manner prescribed in the section of *sharī`*a dealing with *ghanā'im*. Later, during `Umar's caliphate, the military was organized as follows:

1. He initiated army professionals and created distinct battalions or military sectors; he created the army of Palestine, the army of Arabia, the army of Iraq, and so on. These armies formed the Islamic Armed Forces. But reporting to military duties was still mandatory for all Muslims, including women and children, whenever needed.

2. A military record (*dīwān*) was established to keep track of military personnel, their pensions, and their attendance. The record was in the Arabic language, maintained by scribes from Quraysh—`Uqayl Ibn Abī Ṭālib, Makhramah Ibn Nawfal, and Jābīr Ibn Mut`am—in the year 20 H. The reason for creating this record was the close attention given to military personnel and the importance of reporting for duty. It was reported that if an individual did not report for duty, his name would be mentioned in the mosque he frequented, which was not appreciated; Arabs considered such an action worse than a sword wound.

3. A regular pension was assigned to military personnel directly from the treasury house. As we have mentioned, they did not have a stable predetermined pension during the time of the Messenger or during the time of Abu Bakr, nor did the troops reside in designated areas; rather they lived in the city along with the rest of the Muslims, ready for war any time it was ordered. Each military division had a representative who received their pensions and distributed them among the people of each division. The pension was paid from the revenues of their respective state. During Mu`āwiyya's caliphate, the army's pension was terminated and specific dates were set when they would receive a payment, and a number of changes were introduced; the caliph gave equal importance to marine and combat ships. This shift was necessitated by wars against the Romans and the need to protect coastal regions along the Mediterranean Sea. It was reported that the number of battle ships reached 1,700 ships before the occupation of Cyprus.

Professor al-Khedrī, may God's mercy be upon him, said on page 459, vol. 3:

"The expansion of the army received great attention from them (caliphs). The Arabs who fought using the tactic "attack-and-retreat" realized that this method was useless when fighting civilized nations. They organized their battling soldiers into lines linked together so that no one would be left out or move ahead of the troops. The army consisted of a front, which usually started the fighting and discovered the way; a middle (*qalb*) where the leader was; two wings; and a leg. Each of these groups was headed by an *amīr* who received his orders from the leader (*amīr*). The knights were also headed by an *amīr*. The knights usually protected the back of the troops so that the army would not be attacked from behind. They followed the instructions and orders very closely."

Once in the battlefield, the troops followed only the orders of their commanding leader. Generally, the leader of the troops also enjoyed the power to decide on the troops' military as well as financial affairs. He also settled disputes and led the prayers. Sometimes, the leader was restricted to managing military affairs, while settling disputes and leading prayers was delegated to special agents. The troops who were not in the battlefield, like the state guards and security officers, were under the command of the governor of their respective state.

Organization of the Executive Branch

We said earlier that during this period the caliph and governors shared one side of the judicial branch, and judges shared the other. All of them were judges. But the title "judge" was specifically given to individuals who issued legal opinions on civil matters and on matters known as *al-aḥwāl al-shakhṣiyya*. The judge, then, did not rule in matters of *hudūd* and punishment. That was left for the caliphs and the governors unless otherwise indicated and authorized by the caliph. Mu`āwiyya expended the duties of Egypt's judge, Salīm Ibn `Itr, to include wounds (*jirāḥ*). Abdul Malik also shared with his judge, Abu Idrīs al-Aurdī, the duties of settling all sorts of grievances. So, any ruling stated by the caliph or the governor, including execution, cutting hands, or imprisonment, or other corporal punishments, was executed by the caliph, governor, or individuals they appointed. In other words, during the time of the Messenger and during the caliphate of the Companions, there were not specific individuals whose job it was to execute laws. In fact, all Muslims were expected to carry out the law since it was understood as part of the religious command to "forbid evil and enjoin what is good." Al-Sa'ib Ibn Yazīd has said:

During the time of the Messenger and Abu Bakr and in the early part of `Umar's caliphate, we went to the drunker and beat him with our hands, with our shoes, with our feet, and with our cloaks. During the last days of `Umar's caliphate, it was made official to flog the drunker forty flogs; if they continued to transgress, they were flogged eighty.

Al-Katānī also reported in his *book al-Tarātīb al-idāriyya wa niẓām al-ḥukūma al-nabawiyya*, vol. 1 page 313:

Ibn al-Arabī reported that the stating of *ḥudūd* was left for judges; its execution was left for individuals selected by the Messenger of God like Ali Ibn Abī Tālib and Mohammed Ibn Muslimah.

This statement should not be understood to contradict what we have stated, since the judges during the time of the Messenger were also governors whose duties included executing the laws. The executors, then, were individuals appointed for that task and included Ali, Ibn Muslimah, and others. We have also reported before that the Messenger said, after ruling in one case: "Go Anīs to the wife of this man; if she confesses then stone her..." As for the rulings of judges in civil matters, usually there was no need for someone to execute such laws because the two parties generally accepted the ruling and undertook the needed action willingly.

These cases were more like seeking a formal opinion, as explained by Abu al-Ḥasan al-Māwardī, who stated that *qaḍā'* at this age was more of an explanation to ambiguous issues. Once a judge removed an ambiguity, everyone abided by the ruling. If it happened that someone refused to obey the order, then the judge enforced the law, as was the case sometimes where the judge participated in person in executing laws by means of advice or warning. In other instances, the judge sought the governor's support to enforce laws. We have reported examples from this period where Ali decreed and executed laws at the same time. So did Iyās and many others. We also mentioned that not writing a law mandating the governor to cooperate with the judges resulted in governors' reluctance to honor some rulings and weakened judges' authorities. This shift also resulted from a weakening religious moral influence and competition among people for material goods. Thus, there was a greater need for the power to enforce laws, than to have more rulings and decrees. The power of the judge depended on his relationship with the governor. This dependency and need to please the ruler in order to build up this relationship caused most judges to stray or fall prey to corruption.

In conclusion, we can say that the Islamic administration of this period was established on a just foundation. The state's leaders fulfilled their duties successfully, carrying out responsibilities in the fields of legislation, judiciary, and administration. Their troops' victories in the battlefields were as important as their victories in administering the affairs of the state. The best proof of this success was the expansion that permitted the Islamic state to reach far lands in a very short time. In fact, before the end of the first Islamic century (H.), the Islamic state managed to expand to include Arabia, Iraq, Shām, Egypt, North Africa, and Southern Spain. If the civil wars between Ali and Mu`āwiyya and between them and the Khawārij—which caused the death of the most prominent Companions—did not take place, the Islamic state's results would had been even more impressive. But God's infinite wisdom in allowing such destructive civil wars to happen is beyond our comprehension and speculation.

III

The Period of Tadwīn

This period starts at the beginning of the first century of the Islamic calendar. It ends in the middle of the era of the Islamic legislative movement where the claim of the closure of *ijtihād* spread, hence the necessity to imitate one of the preceding *imāms*. This was approximately at the beginning of the fourth century of the Islamic calendar. In fact, the last known independent thinker who had his own school of thought and followers, as far as we know, was Mohammed Ibn Jarīr al-Tabarī (d. 310 H.).

This period is known as the "Golden Age" of the Islamic *Ummah*. It was the age in which Islamic civilization reached its peak in culture, development, maturity, and productivity across all aspects and fields of life. It was during this time that the legislative heritage through which Muslims have been enriched was produced. It was during this epoch that a number of jurists known as *imāms* codified major laws, established the foundation of the Islamic legal philosophy, and established statutes. It was in this age that Islamic jurisprudence emerged as an independent science associated with powerful names that will be remembered forever. It was here where the intellectual and material power of Muslims were integrated to continue expansion and growth in the fields of science and politics. At a time when leaders of Islamic armies were cheering victories and propagating the call of Islam in nations as far east as China and as far west as the Atlas mountains, Muslims scholars in various parts of the world continued to make scientific advancements and produce the best that could be produced, especially in the field of religious sciences. The grand mosques in Madīna, Mecca, Kūfa, Baghdad, Egypt, Qayrawān, and Qurṭuba were all centers of scientific movements that brought about the best scholars and brilliant writings.

As we survey the legislative, judicial, and executive branches, a clearer picture of the activity and maturity of this age will develop.

Legislation during this Period

It is hard to collect all the legislative discussions from this period into an article as concise as this one because they are numerous, and because the task of locating all of them is even harder. For this reason, the attempt before you will be limited to the most important subjects:

1. Individuals who served as legislators during this period,
2. Their procedures and the emergence of the *madhāhib*,
3. The changes in sources of Islamic law,
4. The names of some prominent jurists, and
5. A comparison between this period and the preceding one and general remarks.

Before we start the discussion of these subjects, I will briefly define the meaning of the word *tashrī`* (legislation) and the word *ijtihād* (independent thinking) to clear up a misconception that appeared after the publication of the previous two articles dealing with the time of the Messenger and the time of the Companions.

The word *tashrī`* is said to have two meanings:

The first meaning: to make a primary law.

The second meaning: to explain a law stated as an established primary law.

As for the first meaning, *tashrī`* in Islam is done by none other than God, who initiated the primary law, revealed in His Quran and stated by His Messenger as established proofs. In this meaning, only God can legislate.

As for legislation in the second context, the explanation of what an established legal system says was undertaken by the Messenger's successors: the Companions, the learned successors of the Companions, and those who succeeded them amongst the *imāms* and mujtahids. These individuals did not legislate primary laws; rather, they extracted laws from the texts of the Quran, the Sunna, and that which the legislator established as general rules and proofs. If one of them extracted a law using analogy, for example, then he did not legislate a primary law; rather, he exerted an effort to know the reason behind a stated law. The law, then, remained established, except for the fact that he now participated in determining the primary law's manifestations and defining characteristics, which then served as template for new laws. So, by his effort, it became clear to him that the text contained two steps: the situation in which the law is clear, and how he may participate along to determine the reason behind the law.

The word *ijtihād* also has two meanings:

One refers to the exerted effort to distinguish a law from its proof, whatever that proof may be. That includes all of that which the *mujtahid* understands from the text, and that which he extracts by means of analogy or that which he extracts from the general rules of the legal system. Some of the general rules include: the Discharge of Obligations (*Sadd al-ḍarāi`*), the Avoidance of Discomfort (*Daf` al-ḥaraj*), and the protection of Acquired Interests (*al-Maṣāliḥ al-mursala*).

The second meaning refers to determining a law which has not yet been dealt with in the legislative texts using analogy (*qiyās*) and comparing it to what the legislative texts have already dealt with. *Ijtihād*, then, is equivalent to *qiyās*. Thus the laws resulting from this kind of *ijtihād* are limited to those extracted using analogy. This meaning is what should be understood from the Tradition of Mu`ādh Ibn Jabal: "If I don't find (it) in the book of God or in the Sunna of His Messenger, then I use my own *ijtihād*." The first meaning, nonetheless, is very general, so much so that laws resulting from that process include all the results determined by a *mujtahid* during his study of texts and other sources of law. Generally, in the course of this study, we mean the first meaning.

Legislators of the *Tadwīn* Period

We have explained that after the demise of the Messenger [PBUH], the learned ones among the Companions succeeded him in running the legislative branch. These Companions spread out across the Islamic world as a result of the expansion movement, and in order to spread the call of Islam. But a large number of them stayed in Hijāz.

It became known that in each part of the newly annexed land to the Islamic *Umma*, there was at least one scholar or a group of scholars teaching people the Book of God and the Sunna of His Messenger, exerting their own independent thinking in matters not dealt with in the Book or the Sunna, and serving as legislators for the Muslims of each particular region. The annual season of pilgrimage was an opportunity for them to convene and a chance to exchange views and learn more Traditions. Thus, the legislators amongst the Companions were in touch with each other despite the long distance and primitiveness of transportation.

In all corners of the Muslim world, followers gathered around these Companions. They learned the Quran and the Sunna from them, and watched them issue decrees on new happenings. In short, these followers received part of their teachers' knowledge and memorized some of legislation's and Islamic law's secrets. Later, these students became known as the Followers (*Tābi`ūn*). Some of them actually participated, along with their teachers who were the Companions, in issuing formal legal opinion. Sa`īd Ibn al-Musīb, for example, issued formal opinions in Madīna, where a number of Companions were still alive, and so did `Alqama Ibn Qays, who also served as a judge in Kūfa during the time of Abdullah Ibn Mas`ūd. With the extinction of the Companions, these students became the scholars to whom Muslims turned when they needed a legal opinion.

New students were attracted to the scholars amongst these *Tābi`īn*. They learned from them the Quran, the Sunna, and the rulings of the Companions. These Followers of the Followers (*Tābi`ī al-tābi`īn*), in turn, afterwards inherited their teachers' religious and social positions. In this manner, the people of legislature were layered. Each layer consisted of students of their predecessors and teachers of their successors. Hence, the chain of the legislative movement was linked the same way jurists inherited legislature from generation to generation. Muslims, then, inherited the privilege to turn to these people for formal opinions from one generation to another.

This link would be clearer if one were to take a closer look at historical layers of people who served on the legislature during this period in different parts of the Islamic world.

In Madīna after the Messenger, the people of legislation and formal opinion were numerous. Amongst them were the learned Companions. Most renowned of all, we mention the righteously guided caliphs, `Ā'isha, Obayy Ibn Ka`b, Abdullah Ibn `Umar, and Zayd Ibn Thābit. More decrees were memorized from `Umar and his son, and Zayd Ibn Thābit—who were considered legislative scholars in Madīna—than anyone else.

They were followed by the class of learned *Tābi`ūn*. Amongst the most famous of these, we mention here the seven scholars of Madīna; Sa`īd Ibn al-Musīb, `Ubayd Allah Ibn Abdullah Ibn `Utā Ibn Mas`ūd, `Uwah Ibn al-Zubayr, and Al-Qāsim Ibn Mohammed Ibn Abu Bakr. Kharijah Ibn Zayd Ibn Thābit, Sulaymān Ibn Yāsir, and Abu Bakr Ibn Abdul Raḥmān Ibn al-Hārith Ibn Hishām were also active in Madīna.

The students of the Followers then learned from them and formed the next generation of scholars known as the Followers of the Followers, a group that included Rabī`a Ibn Abdul Raḥmān, nick-named Rabī`a al-Ra'y, Mohammed Ibn Shihāb al-Zahrī, and Yaḥya Ibn Sa`īd.

These scholars then were succeeded by their students, a class which included Mālik Ibn Anas and those who followed him. The genealogy of the Mālikī school of thought, for instance, is defined as being formed by the following names: Mālik Ibn Anas, Rabī`a Ibn Abdul Raḥmān and his followers, Sa`īd Ibn al-Musīb and his Followers, Abdullah Ibn `Umar and his followers, and the Messenger [PBUH].

In Mecca, the prominent scholar of law and jurisprudence and the teacher of the Quran and the Sunna was Abdullah Ibn Abbās. He taught a number of students from the class of the *Tābi`īn*. Most notably amongst them were `Ikrimah—his housekeeper—Mujāhid Ibn Jabr, and `Aṭā' Ibn Abī Rabāḥ.

They in turn taught students from the Followers of the Followers, including Sufyān Ibn `Ayniyya and the keeper of the *Ka`bah* Muslim Ibn Khālid al-Zanjī.

These scholars also taught their successors: Mohammed Ibn Idrīs al-Shāfi`ī, who learned in his early age in Mecca from Muslim Ibn Khālid and Sufyān Ibn `Ayniyya. While in Madīna he learned from Mālik. Then he relocated to Iraq and Egypt and learned from the scholars there as well.

In Kūfa and after the Messenger's demise, Ali Ibn Abī Tālib, during most of his lifetime, Abu Mūsā al- Ash`arī, `Ammār Ibn Yāsir, and Abdullah Ibn Mas`ūd undertook the legislative role and issued formal opinions. But it was Abdullah Ibn Mas`ūd who left an important impact in Kūfa, mostly because when it fell under Islamic rule, Umar Ibn al-Khaṭṭāb sent him to Kūfa in the year 11 H. as a teacher and as a governor. Ibn Mas`ūd then built his house next to the mosque and used it as a school to teach the book of God, what he memorized from the Traditions of the Messenger, and issued formal opinions regarding that which was not addressed in those two sources. He used his personal contacts and friendship with the Messenger and his creative mind in the field of jurisprudence to grow to become the most reliable source in Kūfa and Iraq.

The successors and students of the above scholars, also known as the Followers, learned the principles of *ijtihād* from their teachers previously mentioned. This group included: \`Alqama Ibn Qays al-Nakh\`ī, al-Aswad Ibn Yazīd al-Nakh\`ī, Masrūq Ibn al-Ajda\`, Judge Sharīḥ Ibn al-Ḥārith, and Judge \`Āmir Ibn Sherahbīl al-Sha\`bī.

The class that followed these scholars included their students like Ibrāhīm Ibn Yazīd al- Nakh\`ī, the teacher of Ḥammād; Ibn Abī Sulaymān, who influenced Abu Ḥanīfa al-Nu\`mān Ibn Thābit, thus, according to many legal historians, becoming the pillar of the Ḥanafī school of thought.

The chronological order of the Ḥanafī school of thought can be drawn as follows: Abu Ḥanīfa, Ḥammād, Ibrāhīm Ibn Yazīd al-Nakh\`ī, Ibrāhīm's uncle; \`Alqamah, Abdullah Ibn Mas\`ūd, and the Messenger of God.

In Baṣra, formal opinions were issued by the scholar Companions, including Anas Ibn Mālik and Abu Mūsā al- Ash\`arī.

These scholars then mentored a number of students and taught them the principles of *ijtihād*. The graduates of this class included: Qutāda, al-Hasan al-Baṣrī, and Mohammed Ibn Sīrīn, who in turn taught many others.

In Shām, formal opinions were sought from scholars like Mu\`ādh Ibn Jabal, \`Ubādah Ibn al-Ṣāmiṭ, and Abu al-Dardā'.

The above class of scholars, in turn, mentored a number of students and taught them the principles of *ijtihād*. This group included: Abdul Raḥmān al-Awzā\`ī, who was the scholar of Shām and the contemporary of Abu Ḥanīfa, Mālik, and a number of other scholars of their caliber.

In Egypt, the authority of issuing formal opinions belonged to a number of Companions who participated in the expansion; but only

Abdullah Ibn `Amr Ibn al-`Āṣ resided there permanently and taught Muslims the Book of God and the Sunna of His Messenger. He was the first teacher of jurisprudence and the first legislator in Egypt. He was of Kūfa's Abdullah Ibn Mas`ūd's caliber, or of the caliber of Madīna's Abdullah Ibn `Umar, `Ubādah and of Mu`ādh of Shām.

A number of students succeeded Abdullah Ibn `amr Ibn al-`Āṣ. Yazīd Ibn Ḥabīb was the most famous *muftī* in Egypt. Since his father was from Danqala, Yazīd grew up in Egypt and served as the most sought-after judge and *muftī* for Muslims in Egypt, after his teacher Abdullah Ibn `Amr passed away.

Imām al-Laith Ibn Sa`d and his colleagues succeeded Yazīd, who passed their authority to Mohammed Ibn Idrīs al- Shāfi`ī, who settled with the Abdul Ḥakam clan in Egypt during the last years of his lifetime.

The legislative authority of all these scholars from different generations was not delegated to them by caliphs or governors; rather, Muslims trusted them and considered them capable of issuing formal opinions. This trust was based on the assumption that the individuals who had talked to the Messenger and witnessed most events of the Messenger's period would know more about Islamic law, thus raising them to the level of a legislator. Muslims held the same view about those who succeeded the Companions, as well as those who succeeded the Followers of the Followers of the Companions. In other words, students not only inherited knowledge from their teachers, but they also inherited the trust of Muslims. This trust, nonetheless, was maintained and justified by these scholars' and their students' intellectual capacity and piety. Their decrees were sought regarding any issue regardless of their position: as governors or as the governed.

Even caliphs praised the status of such scholars. Not because they were appointed to issue formal opinions, but because of the respect they earned. `Umar Ibn Abdul `Azīz recommended Yazīd Ibn Ḥabīb whenever people from Egypt came to him with questions, the same way Ibn Abbās recommended Sa`īd Ibn Jābir to the people of the Kūfa who came to him with their questions during pilgrimages. When the Kūfans asked him a question, Ibn Abbās usually replied: "Is not Sa`īd Ibn Jābir among you?" These actions do not indicate that Ibn Jābir was officially appointed. Rather, it indicated respect and trust in his capacity to issue formal opinions.

Two characteristics marked the legislative process after the demise of the scholars of the first generation (Companions) and their immediate successors (Followers):

1. At the beginning of this period, about the first third of the second century after *Hijrah*, every *mujtahid* represented an independent individual. He performed his duties by himself. He did not issue any opinion unless an event happened requiring him to do so. He did not record his rulings or the rulings of others. The people were free to choose any scholar they wished and follow the decree they felt most comfortable with. Thus, differences between these scholars were, in a way, a mercy for the people. Islamic law was neither an art nor a science. Rather, it was a collection of laws derived from the Quran and the Sunna and other decrees agreed-upon by the scholars amongst the Companions. It is possible to add to this collection some of the rulings of one or a group of Companions accepted by the *mujtahids* because of the strength of evidence that usually led to such consensus, without which a collective opinion was not possible. Individuals would return to this collection whenever needed to extract laws concerning matters of worship, transactions, and so on.

2. In the later part of this period, and during the time of Mālik, Rabīah al-Ra'y, Abu Hanīah, al-Thawrīyy Layth Ibn Sa`d, Mohammed Ibn Idrīs al-Shāfi`ī , and Abdul Raḥmān al- Awzā`ī and their contemporaries, new factors caused a change in the legislative process due to differences in what was considered a source of law. For example, some legislators relied on Traditions reported by one individual. Others required continuity in transmission and weighed the authenticity of the Tradition itself. Another group restricted sources of law to the collection of rulings issued by the Companions.

Others rejected the authority of the Companions' Traditions. The differing tendencies in interpreting texts also increased divergence in legislation; some were content with a superficial meaning of the texts. These scholars were later known as the "people of Tradition" (*ahl al-Ḥadīth*). Others did not limit themselves to a superficial meaning of the texts, and they were clustered in a group called "people of Opinion" (*ahl al-Ra'y*).

The differences in considering sources of legislation generated a difference in the means and ways of ijtihād, as well as new principles of and conditions for *ijtihād*. As a result, these groups of legislators became distinct political parties and groups. Each party had its own mujtahids, its distinct opinions, and particular school of thought. The only common factor between them was the general trend and the shared foundations used and respected by all of them. The leader of each party was the oldest amongst its *mujtahids*. The leaders and students then formed what became later a distinct school of thought known as Madhhab.

Abu Ḥanīfa and his companions—Abū Yūsuf, Mohammed Ibn al-Ḥasan, and Zafar Ibn al-Hadhbal—performed independent thinking and issued formal opinions independently. Each of them was an absolutely independent scholar, holding the capacity to extract laws from its sources. Abu Ḥanīfa did not imitate any of his companions in either fundamentals or in the branches of jurisprudence. But after studying with him and standing on the validity of his arguments, his companions elected to collect them and explain their implications. They also amalgamated his opinions with theirs so that they would not end up with a distinct school of thought different from his. The whole of these views, then, was dubbed the school of Abu Ḥanīfa, in reference to their leader and elder.

Similarly, Mālik Ibn Anas and his colleagues Ibn al-Qāsim, Ibn Wahb, Ibn Abdul Ḥakam, and Ashhab formed the Malikī school of thought. And so did Mohammed Ibn Idrīs al-Shāfi`ī and his colleagues, who established the Shāfi`ī school of thought.

Once the legists divided according to their affiliations with these parties and groups, each leader was followed by his companions, who grew competitive with one another. At this stage, scholars were more inclined to favor particular views and prefer certain arguments over others. As a result, a number of debates, oral and written, took place. These debates showed impressive depth and systematic analysis as they addressed various legal, philosophical, and religious issues. This was clear from the recorded debates collected by Mohammed Ibn Idrīs al-Shāfiʿī in his books *al-Umm* and *al-Radd ʿalā Mohammed Ibn al-Ḥasan*. These characteristics were also evident from the writings of Imām Abu Yūsuf in the book where he recorded the issues of disagreement between Abu Ḥanīfa and Ibn Abī Laylā. He mentioned the view of these two scholars, then sided with the opinion of one on some issues and the other on other issues. In some instances, he even offered his own opinion, which differed from both jurists. In *al-Umm*, Al- Shāfiʿī listed the views of *imāms* Abu Ḥanīfa, Ibn Abu Layla, and Abu Yūsuf. He also agreed with one of them sometimes, and expressed his own opinion at other times.

In the book *Siyar al- Awzāʿī*, in the chapter on *jihād* issues, Abu Yūsuf recorded what Abu Ḥanīfa and al-Awzāʿī disagreed upon. Abu Yūsuf also took Abu Ḥanīfa's side in most cases. Al- Shāfiʿī reported the same debates in *al-Umm*, but took the side of Awzāʿī in most matters.

These debates have generated two elements:

1. The domain of *fiqh* increased amongst the legislators, turning Islamic jurisprudence into a well-defined science with its own disciplines and its own methodology. This domain was then directed to extract all extractable laws dealing with that which happened and that which might happen. In other words, jurists now not only provided answers to actual cases, but also issued rulings concerning hypothetical situations. It was said that Abu Ḥanīfa was the first to state laws concerning events yet to occur. It was this new development that created the establishment of the field of *fiqh* and all tendencies associated with it.

2. The above development was the seed from which grew the idea school of affiliations. Scholars became more concerned with justifying the opinions of the founders and the Madhhab than reaching an objective conclusion. This would have been of no harm had it continued as an expression of support based on objective research and led to confirming a particular opinion as was the case with Abu Ḥanīfa, who supported the opinions of his companions by providing valid arguments and explanations that were reasonable and logical. This was the approach of all other leaders of Islamic schools of thought. But this changed, to the point where affiliation dictated a forced acceptance or support and imitation without examining proofs or studying opinions.

It was recorded in *al-Hidāyah* that "people were following the school of thought of Ibn Abbās because of a legislative order issued by the Abbasid caliphs, who published that people should perform the Eid prayers according to the school of thought of their grandfathers. As for the term *madhhab* (school of thought), it was believed to have been used first by Ibn Mas`ūd [RAA]."

In al-Khuṭaṭ, Al-Maqrīzī wrote that when Ismā`īl Ibn al-Yas` al-Kūfī, who supported the termination of trusts (*ibṭāl al-aḥbās*), was appointed judge in Egypt, al-Layth Ibn Sa`d wrote to Caliph al-Mahdī: "O! The Commander of the faithful, you have appointed on us a man who dishonors the Sunna of the Messenger of God behind our backs, although we know that he is honest in dealing with money." The caliph then discharged him.

This use of the power of the caliph to support particular views, or to abuse others based on partisan affiliations, was the first seed planted to paralyze the movement of *ijtihād* and halt the growth of legislative movements. Supporters of each school of thought distanced themselves from the study of the proofs and from extracting laws from them and limited themselves to the sayings of their schoolmasters. They held these sayings in a similar manner as the early *imāms* held legislative texts, to the point where an opinion regarding a particular issue was considered equally valid as a text from the Quran and the Sunna, thus making it beyond the scope of *ijtihād*. Their efforts, then, became sectarian efforts rather than independent *ijtihād*. Because of these changes, legists of this period were divided into factions:

- Absolute independent thinkers, which included the four *imāms*, their like, and the Companions.
- School of thought independent thinkers, who were scholars who compared the decrees of the various schools of thought; they were also called "inter-study."
- Issues independent thinkers, who extracted laws not dealt with by the founders of their respective schools of thought; "inner-studies."
- The people of concordance (*takhrīj*), who stated the reasons (or causes) behind a stated law.
- People of validation (*tarjīḥ*), who recommended a particular narration over another given the authority of its narrator from the point of view of reliability or knowledge.

The Class of Imitators

We will mention our opinion on these factions when we discuss legal materials from this period. We referred to it just now to explain that the legists at the end of this period focused their efforts within their particular schools of thought and limited themselves to the sayings of the *imāms*, not to legal proofs. This decreased the productivity of the legislature and weakened it, although the fountain of legal proofs could not be exhausted. The idea of directing one's efforts to support one school of thought, regardless of its right or wrong opinions, created a trend of dishonest interpretation of texts as well as a reliance on weak *aḥādīth* and a rejection of sound ones. It reached a point where Abu al-Ḥasan al-Karkhī, one of the prominent scholars of the Ḥanafī school of thought, said: "If a text contradicts a saying of our colleagues, then it should be abrogated or interpreted." The gap thus increased between the legists of various schools of thought, to the extent that one could find peculiar decrees taking the time and energies of scholars. An example of this distraction is the following case:

Can a man who follows the Ḥanafī school of thought marry a woman who adheres to the Shāfiʿī school of thought?

The answer was affirmative, using an analogy with marrying a woman who is *Dhimmī* from the people of the Book.

Competitiveness in the field of legislation had good and bad impact on Muslims, which will be clarified when we address the period of imitation.

Legislative Methodology

The legists of the second faction, occupied by the *Tābiʿīn* and the *Tābiʿī al-tābiʿīn*, did not have different legislative plans because they followed the same procedures as their ancestors. Once an event occurred requiring a formal ruling, these jurists referred to the Quran and to the Sunna and examined what was memorized from the Messenger's Companions. If they did not find anything in the previous two sources, they used what they found suitable from this source or they exerted their own efforts and made a ruling. Their disagreements, then, did not fundamentally invalidate the sources and proofs of one another. Rather, disagreements were differences, similar to those among their predecessors, originating from an understanding of the meanings texts, from the need for public well-being, or from the availability of a Tradition to one scholar and not to another. These disagreements were never the kind of disagreements leading to the creation of different schools of thought. These differences were not critical, since sources and legal proofs were the same for all the legists. For these reasons, during the first part of this period, there were not different schools of thought in the sense of antagonistic schools; rather, there existed different points of view.

The legists of the third faction, however, including *imāms* and some jurists before and after them, differed in the procedures of legislation, since they fundamentally disagreed on acceptable sources of legislation. From their various approaches to legislation emerged various opinions, and from their various opinions emerged different schools of thought.

In other words, the *madhāhib* were created once their founders differed amongst each other on the foundations of legislature and their legislative approaches, not as a result of mere differences of opinion on secondary issues. The detailed laws of each school of thought cannot be understood unless one looks at them from within each particular school of thought's framework and from the point of view of the scholars within that particular school of thought. Accordingly, each legal tendency had its own scholars called the *mujtahids* of the *madhhab*, whose responsibility it was to extract laws concerning issues not addressed by their *imāms*, while keeping in perspective the respective schools of thought's general procedures and philosophy for extracting laws. Abu al-Abbās al-Qurṭubī, a Mālikī, wrote in his commentary on Ṣaḥīḥ Muslim:

> *Mujtahids* are two kinds: one is the absolute independent thinker who is free to extract laws from primary sources. There is no doubt that this one will be rewarded for his effort; but it is hard, rather impossible, to find one of them in this time. The second is a *mujtahid* within the school of thought of an *imām*. They are generally the judges of justice of this time. He is bound by the foundation and proofs set by his *imām*. He is able to state his own view only in the absence of a ruling from his *imām's* school of thought. But in case there existed a text, and it is not indicated otherwise, he rules accordingly, and he does not exceed studying that ruling and understanding its aspects. If a Tradition from his *imām* is

contradictory to a text, then he is obliged to study the proofs of the two statements from the point of view of his *imām's* school of thought.

We will explain some of the legislative foundations where the scholars disagreed, then we will proceed to explain their legislative approaches. After that, the procedures of the mujtahids of this period will be clarified, as well as their personal foundations in contrast with their agreement on the foundational legal principles, which are the Quran, the Sunna, consensus, and analogy.

1. Decrees of the Companions

The *mujtahid imāms* first disagreed on the issue of the decrees of the Companions of the Messenger. The Companions left behind many rulings dealing with various matters. The Followers and the Followers of these Followers invested efforts in preserving these rulings and reported them from generation to generation, to the extent that such decrees were sometimes conflated with the Sunna. Should these decrees be considered a source of legislation to which a mujtahid must refer if he cannot find a text in the Quran or in the Sunna, concerning a matter at hand, before ruling on it himself? Or should he use his independent thinking after referring to the Quran and the Sunna, as done by the Companions themselves? And, in very short terms: should the Companions' decrees be ranked above analogy?

There is no disagreement regarding the invalidity of a Companion's saying unless supported by proof, because that is the general principle. Nor is there disagreement on the fact that the ruling of any of the Companions does not constitute authority over another Companion. For this reason, the Companions differed while ruling on numerous things. It is also a given fact that whoever imitates one of the Companions in one ruling may follow another. Commenting on these facts, Iraqīs said:

There was a consensus among the Companions that whoever sought formal opinion from Abu Bakr and `Umar could ask Abu

Hurayrah and Mu`ādh Ibn Jabal and others and may adopt any of the views he wants.

We conclude from here that the opinion of a Companion was not legal proof over any of the other Companions, nor was it legal proof during the Prophet's lifetime.

Regarding the time after that, I will quote some of the sayings of the *imāms* where they expressed their respect to the rulings of the Companions, then proceed to conclude a few things from these statements.

Imām Abu Ḥanīfa was asked about his approach in legislation. He said:

I would use the Book of God if it contains the law. If not, I use the Sunna of His Messenger, which is sound and transmitted through trustworthy individuals. If I do not find [a law] in the Book of God or in the Tradition of His Messenger, then I refer to the sayings of his Companions. I would use what I want and leave out what I do not want, without taking the Traditions of others over theirs. Once I arrive to the Traditions of Ibrāhīm, al- Sha`bī, al-Hasan Ibn Sīrīn, Sa`īd Ibn al-Musīb ... (enumerating a number of the later *mujtahids* from the *Tābi`īn and Tābi`ī al-tābi`īn*), I then, can perform *ijtihād* the same way they did.

It was also reported that he was asked what he would do if his ruling contradicted the Quran. He replied that he would abandon his ruling. When asked about his reaction if his ruling happened to contradict the Sunna, he answered that he would abandon his ruling. Then he was asked about his response if he found that his ruling contradicted that of a Companion, and he also indicated that he would abandon his ruling. Finally, he was asked about his response to discovering that his ruling contradicted that of a *Tābi`ī*. He then replied: "If a *Tābi`ī* is a man, I am too a man."

Faqīh of Egypt once sent a letter criticizing some of *Imām* Mālik's decrees:

The Companions of the Messenger of God offered different rulings concerning a number of things. Had I known that you were ignorant of them, I would have sent them to you. The *Tābi'īn*—including Sa'īd Ibn al-Musīb and his colleagues—also differed greatly. Others after that also disagreed and you have witnessed their disagreements in Madīna and other places. You may remember the leading figures, Ibn Shihāb and Rabī'a Ibn Abu Abdul Raḥmān. The disagreements between Rabī'a and those whom I mentioned above are well known to you since you were present. I have heard your comments on that as well as those from others from Madīna including Yaḥyah Ibn Sa'īd, Abdullah Ibn Umar, Kathīr Ibn Farqad, and another who is even older than Kathīr, whose teaching you disliked so much that you left his class... Despite all that, Rabī'a still has a better, more authentic mind, an eloquent tongue, clear favors, a way into Islam, and an honest love for his brothers in general and for us in particular. May God have His mercy on him, forgive him, and reward him with what is better than his achievements.

Mohammed Ibn Idrīs al- Shāfi'ī wrote in his book *al-Umm*:

Those who are capable of governing or serving as judges should not govern or rule unless with absolute good, and that is the Book and the Sunna, or according to what learned people have decreed via consensus or using analogy with the above.

What can be concluded from the above sayings and other sayings of the *imāms* regarding this matter is that later scholars cannot disregard the decrees of the Companions if they were reached by unanimous consensus. This is attributed to the fact that the Companions witnessed the dawn of Islamic legislation and talked with the Messenger, thus enabling them to understand the secrets of legislation. Their *ijtihād* is, then, closer to the truth. If one chooses to contradict them, then his path is not that of the believers. The fact that the Companions have disagreed on a number of issues is proof that their consensus, if reached, must originate from a sound proof. This reasoning is actually an example of ruling by consensus. As an example, when the emigrant Companions and the

Helpers agreed with Abu Bakr on the sixth as the share for the inheriting grandmother, no *mujtahid* ever challenged that decree.

However, if the Companions decreed differently on a particular issue, then *mujtahids* could choose a ruling they wanted depending on their own reasoning. For instance, when the Companions disagreed on the issue of whether brothers could share the inheritance from their grandfather, Abu Bakr did not give them a share on the basis of the grandfather being a father, while `Umar and Zayd Ibn Thābit gave them shares because he was not the direct father, the *imāms* also later disagreed; Abu Ḥanīfa adopted the first view while Shāfi`ī took the second opinion.

The Companions, in another example, disagreed on a question of "voiding previous divorce" (*hadm al-talāq al-sābiq*). `Umar, Ali, Ubay Ibn Ka`b, and `Imrān Ibn Ḥasīs thought that if a man divorced his wife fewer than three times and did not return to her before the end of her waiting period (`*iddah*) and she married someone other than him, then she returned to him, she should return with what is left of the number of divorces. Ibn Umar and Ibn Abbās, however, ruled that she returned to him as if they exhausted all three non-permanent divorces (*talāq rij`ī*), because the second marriage voided one or three divorces. The first opinion was adopted later by Shāfi`ī and Mohammed Ibn al-Hasan, while a number of other *mujtahids*, including Abu Ḥanīfa and Abu Yūsuf, adopted the second opinion. About this, it was said that the young *mujtahids* adopted the view of the old Companions, and the old *mujtahids* adopted the view of the young Companions.

There shall be no dispute whether the Companions' consensus was used as a proof, nor shall there be a dispute whether the *mujtahids* chose one opinion over another in case of a disagreement between the Companions. The real issue was whether a *mujtahid* could ignore all of the Companions' decrees in the absence of consensus among the Companions, or whether their diverse views should be considered as a consensus on a range of possibilities, hence only one of the presented views should be adopted.

From the statement by Abu Ḥanīfa, "Take from any Companion that which I want and leave out that of any Companion I want without taking another view besides theirs," is clearly leaning toward the second possibility presented above. Ahmad Ibn Ḥanbal agrees with Abu Ḥanīfa. al-Shāfi`ī, however, asserts that *mujtahids* are obliged to follow, with no deviation to other sources, the Book, the Sunna, and the consensus of the learned ones. More evidence is clear from the statement of al-Layth Ibn Sa`d in his letter asserting that Rabī`a al-Ra'y contradicted what was previously stated, and that Mālik and his colleagues disliked that and left his class.

We can conclude from the above that the *mujtahids* had different opinions concerning the decrees of the Companions. This affected the discipline of *uṣūl*/jurisprudence, depending on their admission or refusal of the decrees of the Companions as legal proof. It also led to more branching in some areas of law.

2. The Method of Authenticating Sunna

Although the *mujtahid imāms* agreed that the Sunna, if authentic, is a valid proof in religious matters, and that it is the second source of law after the Quran, they disagreed on how to authenticate the Sunna. Based on this disagreement, some of them accepted *aḥādīth* narrated by a particular source they deemed reliable, and some of them rejected *aḥādīth* that were not reported by their preferred source. These disagreements generated a disparity in the laws.

The Ḥanafī *imāms*, for instance, indicated that the Sunna could be authenticated by means of widespread narration (*tawātur*). That is, a reported Tradition should be narrated by a person or a number of people on the authority of a another person or a group of people whom we could trust were not involved in a conspiracy and lying, or by means of abundance (*shuhra*). That is, a Tradition must be narrated by a just (*`adl*) individual on the authority of a just individual and it should be used by scholars of different states or used by the *mujtahid* Companions and not contradicted or refuted by another Companion. For this reason, one of the principles of the Ḥanafīs was the prohibition of abrogating a Tradition or adding to it unless a *mutawātir* or *mashhūr* Tradition is provided. Abu Ḥanīfa explained this when he said:

If I do not find it in the Book of God, I use the Sunna of His Messenger and the authentic Tradition reported by honest ones.

Abu Yūsuf introduced further explanation in his book *Siyar al-Awzā`ī*:

`Umar—as reported to us—never accepts a Tradition unless he puts the individual who reports it under oath.

Be aware that the number of Traditions increased with time. Scholars did not know these Traditions; they contradicted the Book and the Sunna, so be aware of strange *Ḥadīth*. Adhere to the Traditions narrated by the *Jamā`*ah and those known by scholars, and compare things to the Quran; what contradicts the Quran is not a Tradition of the Messenger.

As for *Imām* Mālik Ibn Anas and his companions, they accepted any Tradition used by the Companion scholars and used by Muslims of Madīna, as long as there was no disagreement on its authenticity. The reason behind this was that the people of Madīna acted the same way they saw the previous generation act, who in turn acted in accordance with the actions of the Messenger's generation. This could be included under the category of "working Sunna." Many times, Traditions were dropped simply because they contradicted the actions of people in Madīna. Refer to page 68 of the letters of al-Layth Ibn Sa`d, mentioned above.

Imām Shāfi`ī and his colleagues required that the Tradition must be reported by a "just" individual on the authority of a "just" individual, in a chain going all the way back to the Messenger. A Tradition was accepted even if the narrators were one person-to-one person.

3. Isolation of Induction

If a law was stated without an explanation for the reasons behind it, a mujtahid could exert his independent thinking to determine the reason. The traditionalists called this *takhrīj al-manāṭ*, which was the foundation of analogy (*qiyās*). They disagreed regarding what could be called *manāṭ*. This disagreement also caused disparity in laws. The *imāms* agreed that laws are introduced to provide for the needs of the people and that not all explanations could be adopted as reasoning for a particular legislation. They also agreed that a law's reasoning must be compatible with the law itself. That is, a law's reasoning must explain the benefit or the harm resulting from implementing the law. They added that simple conformity or compatibility of the law with the concluded reason is not enough to dub the conclusion "reason" (*ʿilla*), because many compatible explanations were rejected by the legislator (*musharriʿ*). Some "other thing" must be met before accepting it as the "reason." This "other thing" was again a point of divergence among Muslim legists; a group that included the Ḥanafī scholars said it was the "effect" (*al-ta'thīr*). That is, the acceptable reason must be "influential," so that the legislator considered it or at least considered it analogous in one of the three ways of consideration.

Another group that included the Shāfiʿī scholars said it was the "imagined" (*al-akhāla*): that is, that which came to the mind of the *mujtahid* when he imagined the description of a reason.

As a result of the above debate, other disagreements concerning "acquired interests" (*al-maṣāliḥ al-mursala*) emerged. Acquired interests were interests not voided or supported by an established law. This was a huge field of controversy.

These were some examples of what constituted an area of disagreement between the *imāms* in the foundation of jurisprudence known as *uṣūl*.

As for their disagreement over method, this was manifested in their division into groups called People of Tradition (*ahl al-ḥadīth*), which included the scholars of Hijāz, and people of opinion (*ahl al-ra'y*), which included the majority of the scholars of Iraq.

These labels do not mean that the scholars of Iraq would not use *Ḥadīth*; but, as we have already reported, their clear statements indicate their use of the Sunna once it was available. The label also does not imply that the scholars of Hijāz did not use their reason; in fact, we have reported that all scholars in Hijāz and elsewhere used reason whenever they failed to find a text. Their guide was always the Messenger of God, who used his own independent thinking and approved the independent thinking of his Companions. The Sunna, therefore, remained a legal source for all of them, and also so remained independent thinking as a tool for legislation for all of them.

The divisions and distinct connotations mean that the scholars of Iraq have encountered many circumstances forcing them to look at laws from a different angle and believe that the laws were articulated for some purpose. This purpose must be the well-being of the public, making it rational, not ritualistic. All laws, then, must be designed to avoid harm, eliminate discomfort, and materialize basic needs for society. The prime source of these laws is God alone, may He be glorified. The uniqueness of the source leads to the uniqueness of the laws; thus, these laws must exhibit a degree of similarity linked together with the same type of reasons without any contradiction or antagonism. Scholars were to follow this trend while extracting laws, because only in the light of these reasons can they understand the texts, distinguish between categories, and extract new laws regarding issues not covered in the fundamental sources. This method ought to be followed even if doing so leads them to misinterpret a text or choose one tradition over a more probable authentic one. For this reason, the first thing a scholar should think about is the understanding of the rationale behind inscribing such a law.

The scholars of Ḥijāz, however, did not face the same circumstances as the mujtahids of Iraq. Therefore, they did not have to adopt the same approach. The first thing they looked at in their cases was the text itself and its apparent meaning. They did not examine the concordance of the laws, nor did they think of the effects of such laws if applied without reasoning. They limited their reasoning to the superficial meaning of the text and questioned their reasoning if they did not figure out the text.

To elaborate more, we will enlist some of the key circumstances that forced the scholars of Iraq to adopt such a trend, and then we will mention a few examples highlighting the different outcomes resulting from the different trends. This will make the two methods crystal clear.

Some of the factors that led scholars in Iraq to apply reason to understand the deep meaning of the texts without limiting themselves to the superficial understanding of it were:

1. The lack of narrated Traditions: This was because the number of Companions who settled in Iraq was very small. We also mentioned previously that when `Umar sent the first group of Companions there, he warned them against excessive narration of *Ḥadīth*, which might distract the people of Iraq from memorizing the Quran. So, in Iraq, only the Quran and a few Traditions—narrated by reliable sources—were available. These texts, if limited to their superficial meanings, did not encompass society's needs and answer all their inquiries. Therefore, the scholars occupied themselves with understanding these texts to include all issues using reasoning and rationale. This was not the case in Hijāz.

2. The environment of Iraq was different from that of Hijāz: The Persian Empire left a civilization in Iraq with all its customs and traditions that differed from the primitiveness and naivety of the Bedouins in Hijāz. The scholars in Iraq were asked for formal opinions regarding new matters that Muslims had never before encountered. Therefore, they used intellect and

reasoning to determine laws. The environment, then, helped develop their capacity to research and reason. In Hijāz, however, most matters during the second century might have occurred during the first century. The fact that most scholars memorized Traditions from the Messenger or from the early Companions kept them from expanding the field using their own reasoning or searching for reasons behind the stated laws.

3. The teacher of *fiqh* and legislation in Iraq was Abdullah Ibn Mas`ūd, who tended to examine interests resulting from implementing laws and to ponder on the reasons. In Hijāz, Abdullah Ibn Umar and Abdullah Ibn Abbās were the scholars of *fiqh* and legislation in Madīna and Mecca, respectively, who were very strict in interpreting the Tradition literally.

The Companion scholars also had two trends in legislation. For example, `Umar Ibn al-Khaṭṭāb considered public interest, then thought about how to materialize it. This was clear from his opinions even during the time of the Messenger, which the Quran later confirmed. He also made several suggestions to Abu Bakr during the latter's caliphate. He again showed the same trend concerning a few issues that faced him once he was selected as the caliph. Space does not permit us to enlist `Umar's *ijtihād* during the time of the Messenger, during Abu Bakr's caliphate, and during his own rule. Therefore, we will limit ourselves to mentioning that `Umar exerted independent thinking and ordered *kharāj* to be taken from the people of Iraq, but he left the land (*al-sawād*) in their hands, taxed the imports and exports, and distinguished between the emigrants and helpers in the due pensions, and more. This was regarding issues not dealt with in legislative texts. As for using independent thinking to understand stated texts, we mentioned that he interpreted some verses differently from his predecessors; God says in chapter al-Baqarah: "Divorce is twice; then one has to keep with goodness or release for betterment." As a result, triple divorce (*talāq al-thalātha*) was possible during the time of the Messenger, during the caliphate of Abu Bakr, and during the first two years of

`Umar's caliphate. Then, he said that some people sped through affairs that they later regretted, and he decided to separate the divorces so that they took place on three distinct occasions, not just one.

God also said in chapter al-Tawbah: "Indeed alms are for the poor, the *masākīn*, those in charge of it; for those whom you intend to soften their hearts, to pay for mistaken killing, to pay for those who are indebted, in the way of God, and for visiting strangers..." `Umar argued that God caused Islam to prevail so that we did not need to soften anyone's hearts with money, and he dropped that share.

God said in chapter al-Mā'ida: "The male thief and the female thief, cut their hand..." Ibn al-Qayyim reported in *a`lām al- Muwaqqi`īn* on the authority of Hātib Ibn Abū Balta`a that some of his father's boys stole a camel from a man from Mezīna. When they were brought before `Umar, they confessed. He summoned Abdul Raḥmān Ibn Hāteb and told him: "The boys of Hātib stole a camel of a man from Mezīna and have already confessed." Then he looked at another man and said: "O Kathīr Ibn al-Selat, go and cut their hands." When he went to execute the order, `Umar stopped him, saying:

"By God, I know that you keep these boys hungry, and you force them to work hard, then they resort to eat what God has forbidden. If it were not for this, I would cut their hands. But I will not do that, and I will fine you a heavy fine that will hurt you." Then he asked: "O Ibn Miznī, how much would your camel cost if you were to sell it?" He replied: "Four hundred'" `Umar then continued addressing Abdul Raḥmān Ibn Ḥātib: "Go and give him eight hundred."

If a researcher were to study the *ijtihād* and opinions of `Umar since his acceptance of Islam until he died, he would find that `Umar gave close attention to establishing justice and to considering the wellbeing of the public while applying reason in order to interpret Quranic and Prophetic sanctions. In doing so, he verified reported Traditions and never accepted one that was narrated by only one individual unless it was supported by two others, because there was no room for division in the authority of *Ḥadīth* but not the case in the matters of *ijtihād*, which was an open field for all. `Umar tended to encourage this diversity of *mujtahids*.

A few Companion scholars adopted the method of `Umar. Zaid Ibn Thābit disagreed with Abdullah Ibn Abbās on the issue of inheritance of a mother, if a wife died and left behind her husband, her mother and her father. Ibn Abbās decreed that the mother would inherit the third and supported his view with the verse: "If he does not have children and his parents inherited him, to his mother shall be the third." Zaid, on the other hand, argued that the principle of inheritance in Islam favors sons over daughters, brothers over sisters, and fathers over mothers. Therefore, if we applied the text literally in this case, the husband would get half, the mother would get third, and the father would get the rest, which is the sixth. Hence the mother would end up with twice as much compared to the father. This was not in accordance with the general principle of laws of inheritance in Islam. For this reason, he assigned for the mother a third of what was left after the husband took his share so that she received one sixth of the initial sum and the father one third. Thus, it was in accordance with the general principle although it was contradictory to the literal interpretation of the text. Ibn Abbās, however, did not give much importance to final results as long as the text was applied. His argument was, "O! Zaid, was there a mention of one third of the rest in the Book of God?"

Abdullah Ibn Mas`ūd followed the path and method of `Umar very closely. He, `Umar, and Zaid Ibn Thābit used to seek one other's counsel. Ibn Mas`ūd was also very trusted by `Umar, to the point that when he was appointed to serve in Iraq along with `Ammār Ibn Yāsir, he [`Umar] wrote to the people of Iraq: "I have sent you Adbulalla Ibn Mas`ūd as a teacher and as a minister, choosing him for you over myself." (In *a`lām al- Muwaqqi`īn* it was reported that Ibn Mas`ūd almost never disagreed with `Umar.)

It is clear then, why the scholars of Iraq would adopt reason as a method. Like their teacher Ibn Mas`ūd, they searched for a logical explanation to existing laws and used pure reason to extract new ones, while endeavoring for justice guided by the teachings of their teacher Ibn Mas`ūd and led by their Imām `Umar Ibn al-Khaṭṭāb.

Sa`īd Ibn al-Musīb and his colleagues from Hijāz, as well as their followers like Ibn Shihāb al-Zahrī and Yaḥyah Ibn Sa`īd followed by Mālik Ibn Anas, all inherited many Traditions from the Messenger as well as decrees issued by the Companions. In addition, they were rarely faced with a matter that their predecessors had not dealt with. Therefore, they were not compelled to study the reasons behind laws, nor were they forced to rely on their intellect. For this reason they were labeled the people of tradition, although amongst them there were people who used the methods of the scholars of Iraq like Rabī`a Ibn Abū Abdul Raḥmān Ibn Farūkh, who was known as "Rabī`a al-Ra'y."

Ibrāhīm al- Nakh`ī, al-Aswad Ibn Yazīd al- Nakh`ī, and their colleagues in Iraq, along with the class of Ḥammād Ibn Abu Sulaymān, followed by the class of Abū Ḥanīfa al- Nu`mān Ibn Thābit, did not have large resources of Traditions of the Messenger and the Companions. Most cases brought before them were all new and different. They relied on study of the Quran and a limited number of Traditions to understand the reasons of established laws, thus enabling them to expand the texts to cover these new issues. They established new foundations, general and specific, for the cases at hand. For this reason, they were known as the people of opinion, although amongst them were individuals who used the method of the scholars of Madīna like al-Sha`bī, who disliked reason and criticized bitterly those who use it.

The Following are instances where the scholars differed:

1. Eid al-Fitr alms (*sadaqat al-fitr*)

All scholars agreed that it was mandatory, but they disagreed on three matters:

1-1. Was the mandated amount one armful (*ṣā`*) of wheat, dates, or barley; or was it a half *ṣā`* of wheat and one *ṣā`* of dates or barley?

1-2. Could flour be used as a substitute for barley and wheat or not?

1-3. Could the cash value of the mandated amount be used as a substitute or not?

As for 1-1, it was argued that a number of *aḥādīth* mandated this type of alms. Abu Sa`īd al-Khudrī was reported to have said:

During the time of the Messenger, we gave it (*Fitr* alms) as one *ṣā`* of food, one *ṣā`* of dates, one *ṣā`* of barley, one *ṣā`* of raisins, or one *ṣā`* of wheat. One day Mu`āwiyya came for pilgrimage or *`umrah* and he addressed people from the pulpit, and part of what he said was that he thinks that two armfuls of Syrian wheat would equal one *ṣā`* of dates. Since then, people did what he said." Abū Sa`īd continued: "as for me, I still pay it the same way I used to do before."

The scholars of Hijāz stated that the mandated rule was one *ṣā`* of the ordinary food of each particular country. They added that the Sunna did not permit less than one *ṣā`*. They considered Mu`āwiyya's view as a mere opinion that could not change the established sanctions.

The scholars of Iraq stated that the mandated amount was a half *ṣā`* of wheat and its like and one *ṣā`* of barley or dates, and so on. The argument was that if it was mandated on an individual one unit of an abundant thing, any substitute must be of the same value. The Tradition is then understood in a way that whatever source of food is used, they all have to be of the same value. In light of this understanding, one may reconcile the opinion of Mu`āwiyya, who indicated that two armfuls of Syrian wheat would equal one *ṣā`* of dates.

Regarding 1-2 and 1-3, the scholars of Hijāz indicated that flour and the value of those indicated items would not suffice as substitutes. They argued that the text explicitly stated grain, not flour or their cash-value.

The scholars of Iraq stated that flour and money could substitute for wheat and barley. They argued that there must be a reason for mandating the charity in the first place. Therefore, a capable individual can provide money of equal value to the stated items to help the poor. There is no doubt that flour is as beneficial as grain. And so is money. The mentioning of dates and barley, they argued, is simply to set a standard for the mandated obligation. It does not mean that they are the only things a poor individual can eat. For this reason, Abu Yūsuf said: "I prefer flour over grain, and prefer money over flour and grain, because that is a better way to provide for the needs of the poor."

2. *al-Muṣrāt*

al-Muṣrāt is the covering of an ewe's udder (mammary gland) to make it collect milk so that buyers would think that it was a milky animal when it is not. The scholars of Hijāz said that if a person decided to return the animal after milking it and discovering that it was not milky, he may do so, but he must give it back with a *ṣā`* of dates. The scholars of Iraq said that he could return it and pay for the amount of milk.

The scholars of Hijāz disagreed and base their objection on a Tradition narrated by Abū Huraira: "If one buys a *muṣrāt* and milks it, he may choose to keep it or return it along with one *ṣā`* of dates, not wheat."

The scholars of Iraq argued that it is a case of guaranteeing the return of a property intact. They added that if one happened to destroy the property of someone else, he could provide its analogous value or its value. The Tradition, they stated, must be understood in light of this general principle. The Messenger mandated that one must return the ewe with a *ṣā`* of dates because these were of the same value, which the seller of the ewe needed to receive as compensation. The scholars from Iraq asserted that the *Ḥadīth* should not limit compensation to dates regardless of the value and price of the milk and dates. These items differed in value from one country to another and from one time to another. So, specifying dates was not a legal rule, rather an estimate of the lost property that ought to be replaced by another of the same value. No more, no less.

3. Ransom (*al-diya*)

God says in chapter al-Nisā': "Whoever kills a believer by mistake must free a believing slave and pay ransom to his family unless they indicate otherwise." The Messenger's Tradition stated that for a killed person, the killer must pay 100 camels. If the victim of a murder is a woman, her *diya* would be half that of the man's. There was consensus among the scholars of Iraq and those in Hijāz that the *diya* of a woman is half that of a man's, but they disagreed on *diya* for dismemberment (*diyat al-atrāf*). The scholars of Iraq said it was similar to the diya of homicide (*diyat al-qatl*); a woman's *diya* was half that of a man's. The scholars of Hijāz said that the *diya* for dismemberment of a woman was equal to that of a man up to a maximum of one third. If it exceeded the third, her *diya* became half. It was reported that Rabī`a Ibn Abdul Raḥmān Ibn Furūkh (known as Rabī`a al-Ra'y) had the following conversation with the leading scholar of Madīna, Sa`īd Ibn al-Musīb:

> Rabī`a : What is the *diya* for one finger of a woman?
> Sa`īd: Ten camels.
> Rabī`a : How about two fingers?
> Sa`īd: Twenty.
> Rabī`a : How about three?

Sa`īd: Thirty.
Rabī`a : How about four?
Sa`īd: Twenty.
Rabī`a : What? As her wounds get worse, her *diya* gets smaller?
Sa`īd: Are you from Iraq or what? This is the Sunna!

In other words, Sa`īd made the *diya* for three fingers 30 because it was smaller than a third of the homicide *diya*, which was 100 camels. Once the lost fingers increased to four, making the *diya* more than one third, her *diya* dropped to half of that of a man's so that for one finger the *diya* became five camels, for four fingers it became 20, and for five fingers it was 25 and so on, until it reached 50 camels for ten fingers. He argued that his source was the Sunna and he did not care if the results made logical sense, nor did he care if it violated fundamentals in estimating the punishment for a specific crime.

The scholars of Iraq however, argued that the severity of the crime should not be a cause for the decrease in punishment. They added that a criminal who cut five fingers off a hand must not have a lesser punishment than someone who cut only three. They considered this a clear violation of basic justice in a system of reward and punishment that must concord with the crime. They concluded that such Sunna mentioned by Sa`īd could not be attributed to the Messenger of God.

4. The scholars of Hijāz decreed that if a dress was made impure by the urine of a boy or by the urine of a girl, it could be purified by washing it without wringing it out in the case of the boy's urine. But it must be washed and wrung out in the case of the girl's urine. They supported this by a *Ḥadīth*: "rinse out the urine of the boy and wash out the urine of the girl." Scholars of Iraq saw no difference and stated that the clothes must be washed (rinsing and wringing out) in either case, because human urine was not pure and there was no difference between female urine and male urine. The

general rule in cleaning is to do necessary actions until one thinks that the impurity is gone. This can be accomplished by rinsing or washing in either of the cases. They argued that the distinction between the two was not based on logical reasons. While taking this stance, they doubted the authenticity of the Tradition altogether, or they linked it to a specific case that had particular circumstances.

There is a lot to say in this regard if we continue down this avenue. A look at the books of fiqh enlisting differences from one school of thought to another and their various arguments would clarify this issue further. It suffices to mention *al-Badā'i`* and *Fatḥ al-qadīr*, in which one may notice that the people of opinion amongst the *mujtahids* did not reject a Tradition if it existed, but they tried to understand it in a way that agreed with the *`illa* of legislation and its general principles, even if their attempt to understand it appeared to be a sort of interpretation. The people of tradition, on the other hand, did not ignore logical reasoning but did not rely on reasoning to understand a *ḥadīth*. They were satisfied with the superficial interpretation of a text, even if that understanding was thought to lead to an illogical end.

These two trends had their own views. On the one hand, the method of Hijāzīs protected the texts and prevented any alteration of them. There were many cases where interpretation alienated texts from their true intent. On the other hand, the method the Iraqīs adopted widened the field to materialize the interests of the people and established a rational understanding of the texts, thus reconciling between the texts' true intent and what was dictated by reason. Islamic legislation benefited greatly from both methods, both of which influenced it positively.

Those who accuse scholars of Iraq of following their whims and their own desires are no different from those who label the people of *Ḥadīth* as being short-sighted, saying that these people do not use their brains and do not know anything. The truth is that both schools, the Iraqi school and the Hijāzi school, have contributed to the legislature. Mohammed Ibn al-Ḥasan, a friend of Abū Ḥanīfa, wrote in the book *Adab al-qāḍī*:

> There is no correct *Ḥadīth* without opinion and there is no correct opinion without *Ḥadīth*.

As validation for this statement, we report that Mohammed Ibn Idrīs al- Shāfi`ī drew on both schools and debated scholars from both camps. His *ijtihād* could be classified as one that belonged to either school depending on the case at hand.

From the above explanation, it should be clear by now that the different schools of thought are not born of different decrees concerning secondary issues. Rather, they were formed as a result of fundamental differences concerning methodology. These differences in method resulted in distinct decrees. These differences were mostly centered on questions like these:

Can one disregard the decree of a Companion concerning a particular case or not?

Is a *tawātur* or *shuhra* of a Tradition required for it to be used for legislative purposes or it is not required?

Is a description of the legislative reason on which a legal proof is based required or not?

And, finally, should a text be understood in the light of reason, even if that leads to contradicting its literal meaning; or should it be understood literally, even if that leads to antagonizing reason?

The above are just samples of the fundamental issues that gave rise to the different schools of thought. These differences generated other differences on the level of secondary legal matters. Some of the scholars of each school of thought gave close attention to differences between their *imāms* and those who disagreed with them. They also tried to extract the foundation and the method of their *imāms*. The results were used to determine that the differences between particular scholars are fundamental differences, not mere disagreements on secondary issues, to help them understand these laws, and concord the laws in a systematic way as set by each school of thought.

Among the people who have done this, we mention the Ḥanafī scholar Abu al-Hasan al-Karkhī (d. 340 H.). Al-Karkhī collected 35 fundamental qualifications, classified starting with the first qualification: "What has been proved by certainty (*yaqīn*) cannot be abrogated by doubt (*shakk*)."

Abu Tāhir al-Dabās collected 17 fundamental qualifications which he labeled: *madār ijtihād al-ayimma* (The domain of *imāms'* independent thinking).

Imām al-Dabbūs collected a number of fundamental qualifications in his book: *Ta'sīs al-nadhar*. He added that the Ḥanafī scholars themselves disagree on these qualifications the same way they differ from scholars of other schools of thought. He organized his work in a way where he first introduces a qualification, then he enlists the diverging opinions that stem from it.

Great work was done by the author of *al-Ashbāh wa al-nadhā'ir*, in which he categorized these qualifications.

Amongst the Shafi`īs, a number of scholars have done similar work including Tāj al-Dīn al-Sabkī, as reported in *al-Ashbāh wa al-nadhā'ir*.

The author of *al-Madkhal ilā madhhab*, al-Imām Ahmad Ibn Ḥanbal, along with many other scholars from the Ḥanbalī school of thought, also collected qualifications.

The foundations of these schools of thought and their specific rules were also introduced in the section of secondary laws and their proofs.

In my opinion, if the particular foundation of legislation of each school of thought were to be studied along with the secondary laws that branch out from it and compared to each other, that would have great effect on developing the capacity of *fiqh* and shed light on the laws, thus making them more comprehensible.

Changes in Legislative Sources

The first legislative source:

The first legislative source is the Quran, which was never changed, and it remains a mandating proof and the prime source and reference by Islamic legislators. All those who served in the legislature refer to the Quran as soon as a case is brought before them. If he finds a text, he applies it. He does not have any other alternative except his extra effort to understand the text and to comprehend its implications.

There is a general consensus among Muslims that the laws of the Quran are to be followed and that it is not permitted for a Muslim to ignore them at a particular time or in a particular place. There was no disagreement on this issue between one scholar and another. However, they disagreed on the meaning of some verses. One scholar might understand an imperative to mean a command, a particular as a general, a generic to mean an absolute, or a text to mean literal meaning. Another scholar might understand an imperative as a preference, a general as a specific, a generic as limited, and a text as its interpretation. Each of them would use hints and evidence to support his understanding. These differences are not a debate over the validity of the verses but are disagreements over its implications, because they all agree on its validity as a legal proof (*dalīl shar`ī*).

In respect to the Quran we mention two things:

1. The words of the Quran were fixed and its publication was standardized.
2. The availability of commentaries to explain the meaning of its verses and to enlist the reasons of revelation of some verses.

Regarding the first point, we add that that process secured it from any alteration or change. It is a fulfillment of God's promise: "Indeed it is We Who have revealed the *dhikr*, and it is We Who will protect it." The fixing of the wording of the Quran was done in two ways:

1-1. The increase in number of individuals who memorized the Quran, and its widespread teaching: People used to compete in memorizing the Quran to the point that in each state one could find large numbers of people who had memorized the whole Quran. Muslims inherited this practice generation after generation regardless of race or national background. Of the most famous memorizers of the Quran, from whom many other Muslims learned it, we mention the seven readers (*al-Qurrā' al-sab`ah*); Nāfi` Ibn Abū Na`īm in Madīna, Abdullah Ibn Kathīr in Mecca, Abu Umar Ibn al-`alā' in Basra, Abdullah Ibn `āmir in Damascus, and Abu Bakr `āṣim, Ḥamzah Ibn Habīb and al-Kasānī in Kūfa. All of these memorizers passed away in the second century *Hijrī*. They passed their gifts to their students, who have passed them to their successors, and so on, thus creating a chain of *huffāẓ* (memorizers), who initiated the recital of Quran as a science dubbed "science of recitation" (*`ilm al-tajwīd*). This practice was enforced by the belief that memorization of the Quran is the best form of worship.

1-2. The introduction of vowels into the Quran and the artistic style of vocalizing its verses: We have indicated before that the Quran was written down during the time of the Messenger, but on loose sheets. Some of these copies were left with the scribes of the Quran, and some were kept with the Companions, who wrote it for him. We have also mentioned that Abu Bakr gathered these sheets together, and then later Uthmān copied from this collection and distributed it in the Islamic states to be kept in the grand mosques. The Book as we have it today is named after Uthmān, since he was the one who collected and distributed it.

But the style of writing the Quran then was in the Kūfī style, which did not include the vowels, diacritics, or short and long vowels. The written language was, in a way, one that did not distinguish between *`inda*, *`adbun*, and *`ibādun*. One cannot see the difference between *Yakhda`ūn* and *Yukhādi`ūn* or "*Fatabaiyyanū*" and "*Fatathabbatū*." All three examples would have the same consonantal skeleton.

At first, this potential source of confusion was not a problem, because the practice of memorizing the Quran and its oral transmission minimized the effect of the problem of the written Arabic. Most readers followed what was on the lines but read what was in their hearts. None of the readers ever relied on the written script only.

But once many non-Arab communities converted to Islam and writing the Quran spread among individuals, it was feared that non-Arab speakers would influence the pronunciation of the Quran of those readers who did not memorize it. To solve the problem of pronunciation, the governor of Iraq, Ziyād Ibn Aybah, appointed Abu al-Aswad al-Du'lī, who was one of the great Followers who had memorized the Quran, to put symbols in order to help people read the Quran. He started by vocalizing the endings of the words. He put a dot on top of the letter to indicate the accusative marker (*fatḥa*), a dot below the letter to indicate genitive marker (*kasra*), a dot to the side of the letter to indicate the nominative marker (*ḍamma*), and two dots to indicate *tanwīn*.

To solve the problem of confusing the letters and the motions, the other Governor of Iraq, al-Ḥajjāj Ibn Yūsuf, appointed Nasr Ibn `Āṣim to work on the problem. He then introduced the single dots and the paired dots.

Al-Khalīl Ibn Ahmad later changed the symbols of Abū al-Aswad; he made the *fatḥa* a horizontal line on top of the letter, the *kasrah* a small the Arabic letter, *yā'* shaped, and the *dhamma* to small *waw* on top of the letter. He did not only put vowels on top of the endings of the words, but he also vocalized the entire word. He also added the symbols of long motions as well as the symbols for the energized letters (*tashdīd*). The Quran has been copied the same way since. Later, writing the Quran emerged as an independent "science" of writing distinct from regular writing styles.

Regarding commentaries and interpretations, Mohammed Ibn Jarīr *al-Ṭabarī* recorded the reported commentaries on the Quran. He also collected the Traditions and commentaries of the Companions and Followers. A number of commentators followed him and put forth their own works. Some of these works focused on the eloquence and miraculous aspects of the Quran. Others went on to interpret the Quran.

What is of importance to us as we deal with legislation here is that scholars commented heavily on legislative verses. They even wrote special works dubbed "the Laws of the Quran," which were indexed by Ibn al-Nadīm to include: *Ahkām al-qur'ān* by *Imām* al-Shāfi`ī, *Ahkām al-Qur'ān* by Abū Ja`far al-Taḥḥāwī, and *Ahkām al-Qur'ān* by al-Haṣṣāṣ. Other scholars followed their lead and wrote their own commentaries. These initiatives were wise decisions and constituted a great service to the field of Islamic law. The commentaries constituted a valuable reference and a rich tradition used by all scholars of the various schools of thought. Based on this work, new laws were extracted. But as far as we know and from the old books we have seen, the oldest commentary I have read is the book of *al-Ḥaṣṣāṣ*; it is clear that many of these commentators approached legislative verses from a sectarian position, hence these books were nothing more than sectarian work, not commentaries on the foundations of various schools of thought. I have read some of the books that start by mentioning the verse followed by a list of the different opinions of the schools of thought. But there is no abstract interpretation of the verses as they are without referring to the views of the various schools of thought. Because of this, in my opinion, the commentaries of this period were nothing more than *fiqh* discussions.

The second legislative source

The second legislative source is the Sunna. A few things happened to the Sunna during this period:

1. The collection and writing of the Sunna.

2. Its adoption by the Followers and the debate over whether it was an independent source of legislation.

3. The debate between those who accepted it as a legal proof.

We will proceed to clarify the above points then conclude with our own views on this subject matter.

The Recording of the Sunna

We previously mentioned that the Sunna was not written down during the time of the Messenger of God. We indicated that the Messenger chose scribes to write down the Quran as they heard it from him, but that he did not do the same for the Ḥadīth. In fact, he ordered them not to record his sayings. Therefore, up until the end of the first century, there was no other written source of legislation except the Quran. The Sunna was never recorded at this stage, except for a few sayings recorded by a small number of Companions, who did so for their personal use as reported by *mujāhid*, who said:

> "I have seen with Abdullah Ibn `amr Ibn al-`Āṣ a written journal. I asked him what it was, to which he replied: "*al-Sādiqa*! containing what I have heard in person from the Messenger of God [PBUH]."

We mentioned that the idea of recording the Sunna was mentioned to Caliph `Umar Ibn al-Khaṭṭāb, but this suggestion was not undertaken by `Umar for fear of confusing it with the Quran. It was also repeated again before Caliph Umar Ibn Abdul `Azīz, a decedent of `Umar Ibn al-Khaṭṭāb, in the second century *Hijrī*. He wrote to the governor of Madīna, Abu Bakr Ibn Ḥazm:

> "See what is left of the Tradition of the Messenger of God and write it down. After all, Abu Bakr started recording the *Ḥadīth*."

He also ordered Shihāb al-Zahrī to study the *Ḥadīth* of the Messenger of God and collect it in books to be distributed in the Islamic states. After this order, the second source of legislation became recorded and written down to be referred to whenever needed. Before that, the Sunna was only memorized and transmitted orally. Once recorded, it was secured from any attempt at change, addition or deletion. Once the second source of legislation was fixed, it was not possible to resort to analogy without referring to it first.

However, the collection and recording of the Sunna was not done the same way the Quran was recorded. After copying the Quran from its original copy, Uthmān ordered all other written versions to be burned. Hence, the copies in all states were identical. The Sunna, on the other hand, was never standardized and already-existing copies were never burned. For this reason, the Sunna remained different from one scholar to another.

Abu Ja`far al-Manṣūr, the second Abbasid caliph, noticed this problem but did not manage to take necessary measures to standardize the Sunna. It was reported that Abu Ja`far al-Mansūr ordered Mālik Ibn Anas, the scholar of Madīna, to write a book for the people to avoid the easiness of Ibn Abbās and the strictness of Ibn Umar. Ibn Anas responded by writing *al-Muwaṭṭa'*. He then tried to force the people to accept *al-Muwaṭṭa'* the same way they accepted Muṣḥaf Uthmān, but Mālik told him: "It is not possible, because the Companions were divided after the demise of the Messenger; each one followed what he heard." After hearing this, al-Manṣūr changed his mind.

At any rate, the recording of the Sunna had a positive effect even though it did not unite the community on one single legislative source as the Sunna.

We don't know of any surviving documents dating before the work of Abu Bakr Ibn Hazm and Mohammed Ibn Shihāb. The oldest material we have seen is *al-Muwaṭṭa'* by Mālik Ibn Anas, in which he amalgamated the Traditions of the Messenger with those of the Companions and Followers. He used the ascription method (*masānīd*), where one first mentions the narrator then enlists all *aḥādīth* reported by that particular narrator. The collection by subject is called the assorting method (*taṣnīf*). Most of the *masānīd* were written in the later part of the second century *Hijrī*. The oldest *musnad* we have seen is that of *Imām* Ahmad Ibn Ḥanbal.

The third generation found in these documents' large resources, so they resorted to filtering the reported materials. We mention the most prominent of them, al-Bukhārī (d. 256 H.), Muslim (d. 261 H.), Abū Dawūd, al-Tirmidhī, al-Nasā'ī, and Ibn Mājah, all of whom died in the third century *Hijrī*. Their books are known as The Six Sound Books (*al-Ṣiḥāḥ al-sitta*).

Close attention was not only given to writing and categorizing the Sunna, but also to studying the chain of narration from the point of view of accuracy, justice, and soundness. The people who undertook this task were known as the people of *al-jarḥ wa-'l-ta*`dīl (examination and correction). The study of the Sunna then became twofold: transmission (*riwāya*) and knowledge (*dirāya*), fields that were well-studied and researched by scholars. This effort generated new sciences in the field of *Ḥadīth* the same way sciences were created in the field of the study of the Quran.

The Adoption of the Sunna as Legal Proof

During the time of the Messenger and that of the Companions, there was no dispute over the validity of the Sunna as a legal proof.

It was considered the second source after the Quran. Ibn Jabal stated, as we indicated, that he would use the Quran, the Sunna, then exert his own *ijtihād*. Abu Bakr also asked the people if there was anyone who memorized something from the Messenger whenever he was faced with a case not addressed in the Quran. And so did `Umar and the rest of the legislators amongst the Companions and Followers. The supportive text in this regard was God's words: "O you who believe, obey God, obey the Messenger..." and "And if they refer it to the Messenger and the learned ones..." and "If you dispute some matter, refer it to God and to the Messenger..." and "Whoever obeys the Messenger, has obeyed God..." etc... Because of this explicit proof no one ever argued against the validity of the Sunna as a mandated legislative proof.

By the end of the first century *Hijrī*, however, with the extinction of the Companions who were capable of distinguishing lies from the *Ḥadīth*, profiteers made up *aḥādīth* to legitimize their actions and cover up their mistakes. The fact that the Sunna was not collected and written down made it very easy for them to do so. As a result, the number of *aḥādīth* increased and contradictions appeared, causing the rise of slander and defamation. It became very hard to distinguish between sound *aḥādīth* and those which were not sound or authentic. Furthermore, since the Companions did not require that *aḥādīth* were reported verbatim as said by the Messenger, the possibility of misinterpreting a *Ḥadīth* was very probable.

Because of these two reasons, along with some other reasons, scholars were divided over the question of whether to use the Sunna as a legislative proof.

A group of scholars rejected the Sunna in its entirety. This group evolved in Basra, where *i`tizāl* was created. They argued that God revealed the Quran, which contained the explanation of everything, so how could one interpret obligations and commands set forth in the Quran, or limit the general laws or generalize a specific law using *aḥādīth*, when we are not absolutely sure of its authenticity, nor are we sure about the infallibility of its narrator? They added: How can a thing believed to be absolutely authentic (Quran) be explained by something that is probably authentic (the *Ḥadīth*)?

In my opinion, this was a weak argument, if not absolute deviance. Because God—may He be glorified—has only entrusted to people tasks that they can handle. Concerning the Tradition, all that can be done is to use all possible means to maximize their assurance about its authenticity and minimize doubts of its inauthenticity (*taghlīb al-ẓann*). One who manages to establish a high probability that a Tradition was said by the Messenger of God is required to live according to that Tradition. Were absolute certainty about the authenticity of a Tradition required as a condition, no judge would ever be able to take any statement from a witness, nor would the prayer of a Muslim be considered valid, because the statement of a witness is nothing more than the most probable opinion. Facing the Qiblah is also established on the best approximation of orientation toward the Ka`ba. The effort of the scholars of the Sunna in examining and verifying it leads to the increase of its probable authenticity.

I wonder how can those people who have rejected the Sunna in its entirety perform their prayers, pay the alms, fast, or perform pilgrimage! According to their misguided teachings, when God says "establish your prayers" (*aqīmu al- ṣalā*), it suffices the Muslim to perform what the word "*ṣalā*" means even once in a lifetime. The five prayers, the determined number of prayer units (*rak*`a), and the established way of practices, none of that is necessary if we are to adopt their logic. The same applies to alms, pilgrimage, fasting, divorce, marriage, trade, and usury, everything mentioned in the Quran in general terms and detailed by the Messenger as inscribed by God: "We have revealed to you *dhikr* so that you may explain to people what has been revealed for them."

Another group refused to use the Sunna that was not corroborated by the Quran as a legal proof. They argued that whatever Sunna explaining the Quran is supplemental to the Quran and is a valid proof like the Quran. They add that God has provided the Messenger with the capacity to explain, thus, his explanation is supplemental to what has been legislated in general terms in the Quran. The explanation (*bayān*), therefore, is a proof against or for Muslims. The content of this opinion is that the Sunna is not an independent source of legislation, and any part of it that contains prohibition or legalization not supported in the Quran, not explaining the general statements of the Quran, cannot be used as a proof.

This is a wrong and illogical view because if a Tradition has been determined to be that of the Messenger of God, then it must be a proof because its source is infallible, not because its content is an explanation of that which is in the Quran.

It is ironic that people who hold this view would use an authentic *Ḥadīth* explaining alms from money and gold. They stated that mandatory alms were that which were mentioned in the Sunna. But even if the same method of authenticating the first *Ḥadīth* was used and authenticated, the *Ḥadīth* forbidding the eating of the meat of domesticated donkeys, and wolves and birds, and all that which was stated in the Sunna only—they still would not use it, and it would not be used against them, even though both Traditions come from the same source and were reported by the same authority. Once these people realized that this distinguishing is not reasonable, they asserted that all that which is stated by the authentic Sunna is in fact an explanation to what has been stated in the Quran in general terms. The Messenger, then, either explained generalized verses, or used analogy to extract general principles from the Quran. For example, he legalized what would be detailed from "He made legal for them *ṭayyibāt*" and prohibited what would be detailed from "And He prohibited on them *khabā'ith*." There is nothing in the Sunna that could not be traced back to its root in the Quran, which could be general or specific laws.

The majority of Muslim scholars hold the view that the authentic Sunna is a religious proof, whether it is a saying, an action, or tacit approval. The Quran, and actions of Muslims since the dawn of Islam, are proof that could be disputed only by someone who is arrogant. Those who say that Islam is the Quran alone are making a contradictory statement, because the Quran contains a number of verses mandating the obedience to the Messenger and the referral of Muslims' affairs to him. The messenger was also appointed as a role model. How could one accept all these commands while rejecting his decrees and his legislation? For the above reasons, some scholars have said that when the *khawārij* fabricated the *Ḥadīth*, "any *Ḥadīth* that reaches you from me, test it with the Quran; if it does not contradict it, then accept it..." Some people said, "We have tested this *Ḥadīth* with the Book of God and found it contradictory to the Quran. Because the Book of God has mandated the obedience of the Messenger and following only his authentic Sunna."

Although the majority of the *imāms* agreed that a Sunna is a legal proof once it is established as authentic, they however disagreed on the method of authenticating it. Some used the Sunna as a proof for a law not mentioned in the Book only if it is *mutawātir* or *mashhūr*. Others used the sound Tradition that is narrated by a just individual even if he is just one person. We have mentioned this before and concluded that it is a disagreement over the method of transmission, not a disagreement over its validity as a proof.

As for the third source for legislation, analogy (*qiyās*), it was the subject of the scholars' research and the strongest factor that contributed to their divergence.

We have mentioned on many occasions that the scholars amongst the Companions during and after the time of the Messenger used analogy to extract laws not mentioned in the Book or in the Sunna. They also used general principles of legislation and proofs mentioned by the legislator (*shāri`*). For these reasons, most of their rulings were justified by their desire to eliminate discomfort (*daf` al-ḥaraj*), avoid harm (*daf` al-ḍarar*), or establish justice (*taḥqīq al-`adāla*), and so on, as established in the principles of Islamic legal theory and its aims.

Ijtihād of scholars at this age was unrestricted, free of any conditions. The domain of *ijtihād* extended because of the soundness of the scholars' temperaments, their understanding of the essence of legislation, and their commitment to realizing the welfare of the public. At this time, the absolute freedom of the scholars did not represent any danger since they were known, in contact with one another, and exchanged opinions. We have seen that Abū Bakr did not make his own decisions until after he sought the counsel of anyone knew who had any Traditions from the Messenger of God. So did `Umar and those who adopted their methods. If they did not find any Sunna, they used their judgment in the light of spirit of Sharia and its general principles.

After this age however, absolute freedom in the field of *ijtihād* appears to have had an unexpected outcome, because the narrators of Sunna relocated abroad to various Islamic states, and it became hard to know if there was any Sunna concerning a particular matter. It became possible that a scholar could exert his independent thinking in a matter already addressed in the Sunna. Issues taken into consideration before making a ruling became numerous. Also, it was possible that the mujtahid saw an apparent reason and need but failed to see others who were more important to the legislator. We should mention also that the number of *muftīs* had also increased dramatically with time.

The domain of *ijtihād*, as well as its regulations, was established during this period due to fears that the absolute freedom of independent thinking could lead to ignoring legislative texts, considering issues ignored by the prime legislator, or having in the field individuals who were not qualified. They mandated that independent thinking in matters not addressed in the two sources must be done through analogy: that is, by comparing two issues that share the same legislative reasons. They also inscribed that the legislative reason on which analogy was based must be a physical description conforming to the law inscribed by prime legislator and possibly considered by him. This research in the Book and the Sunna dealing with the way of extracting laws form the foundation of the science of fundamentals of jurisprudence or Islamic legal theory (*`ilm uṣūl al-fiqh*). The first people who wrote on this subject, as far as we know, are Abu Yūsuf, Mohammed Ibn Ashāb Abū

Ḥanīfa, and Mohammed Ibn Idrīs al-Shāfiʿī. We will expand on this when we talk about the results of legislation.

From here on, the domain of *ijtihād* decreased and sometimes became incapable of providing for the welfare of the people. Once scholars felt this limitation, they resorted to state what was preferred, to the extent that we can see some laws stated as follows: "The contract is void by analogy, permitted by preference (*istihsānan*)." The preference mentioned here is nothing but a reversion to the freedom of ijtihād that existed during the early part of the first period.

Limiting the extraction of laws by analogy did not eliminate the danger, and did not prevent some scholars during this period from studying the foundation of this proof. Baṣra, the homeland of theologians (*mutakallimūn*) and people of opinion and debate, was the birthplace of this study. In it was born the Muʿtazilī trend. This started the claim that Sunna is not a religious proof. And in it grew the idea of rejecting analogy as a religious proof. There was a debate between those who had rejected analogy and those who had accepted it as a religious proof, where each side presented its argument and evidence to support their view and refute the other. It was during this time period that *Imām* Dawūd Ibn Ali, known as Dawūd al-Ẓāhirī, who was born in Kūfa in the year 202 H. and who grew up in Baghdād, appeared. He learned *fiqh* from al-Shāfiʿī and was one of his brightest students. He created his own school of thought, based on the rejection of analogy and which restricted extraction of laws to the literal interpretation of the Book and the Sunna. He supported his views by introducing evidence from the primary sources of law. His son and his friends adopted his method, which became one of the Islamic Schools of thought during the middle of the fifth century *Hijrī*.

Those who want to know the extent of this debate and the efforts of both sides may read *al-Risāla* and *al-Umm* by Mohammed Ibn Idrīs al- Shāfiʿī. One may also read what was reported about Dawūd Ibn Ali, the leader of the Ẓāhirī school of thought, and vol.

2 of *a`lām al-Muwaqqi`īn* by Ibn al-Qayyim, all of which contain what would satisfy the desire of the researcher.

The people who rejected analogy usually used two arguments:

1. If one were to examine the laws of Sharia, he would notice that it is not systematic; it distinguishes between analogous rules, yet it generalizes to include conflicting rules. Anything that is of that nature is beyond the atmosphere of rationale, but entrusted to us by God. We have to conform because He cannot be asked for the reason of His deeds. (Ibn al-Qayyim enumerated examples in which the legislator distinguished between similar things and generalized over different things and he explained their context.)

2. Analogy is based on opinion (*ẓann*), because the extraction of reason from the text (*takhrīj al-manāṭ*) is based on opinion. The polishing of the reason by eliminating some of the descriptions and considering others (*tanqīḥ al-manāṭ*) is also based on opinion. All of the steps of the analogists are based on opinion, which does not provide the truth. As God says: "Do not say what you do not know."

Those who accept analogy present two arguments:

1. The texts are limited, whereas the matters and issues are neither limited nor finite. A limited source cannot be the only source for what is unlimited because that would cause discomfort. God did not institute discomfort to the people in his religion. To eliminate this discomfort, the legislator made analogy one of the proofs so that one can extract new laws regarding issues of different times. The claim that laws are ritualistic is false and was rejected by many legislative verses and *aḥādīth*. The claim that the steps of analogy are based on opinion does not need to be answered because God does not entrust to people anything beyond their capacity. If they cannot afford anything better than opinion, so be it. If certainty were a condition, many laws and actions of worship would have stopped.

2. The Messenger [PBUH] used analogy and grouped similar issues with one another. For instance, he prohibited the simultaneous marriage from a woman and her father's sister or her mother's

sister using analogy with God's prohibition of simultaneous marriage with the two sisters. He also stated the reason for this prohibition: "If you do that, you cause discontinuity in the blood relation." There are more examples where the Messenger used analogy. The Messenger also approved the statement by Mu`ādh Ibn Jabal when he said: "If I don't find a text I will think on my own." Abū Bakr and `Umar also used their independent thinking whenever they failed to find a text and none of the prominent scholars from the *muhājirīn* and *anṣār* ever objected. The total rejection of analogy is wrong and it is contradictory to the consensus of the Companions during the dawn of legislature.

During this period, legislators did not limit themselves to extracting laws for secondary issues, but they also gave considerable attention to the foundation of extracting laws and the sources of legislation. They examined it from all angles. By the lapse of their age, *fiqh* and legal theory were developed to become two disciplines of materials rich for science as if they did not leave for those after them any space to fill and forcing them to live as parasites; nurturing from their work. The most obvious example of this dependency is the claim that the doors of *ijtihād* were closed, which spread amongst them. You might have seen in the section of the results of legislation of this period the most famous of that which they have left in the fields of *uṣūl* and *furū`*.

INDEX

www.ingramcontent.com/pod-product-compliance
Lightning Source LLC
Chambersburg PA
CBHW032057020426
42335CB00011B/373